D0852737

THE HEADLESS GHOST

WILLIAM E. WARREN

THE HEADLESS GHOST
True Tales of the Unexplained

Illustrated by Neil Waldman

Prentice Hall Books for Young Readers
A Division of Simon & Schuster Inc.
New York

Text copyright © 1986 by William E. Warren
Illustrations copyright © 1986 by Neil Waldman
All rights reserved including the right of
reproduction in whole or in part in any form.
Published by Prentice Hall Books for Young Readers
A Division of Simon & Schuster Inc.
Simon & Schuster Building
Rockefeller Center
1230 Avenue of the Americas
New York, NY 10020

10 9 8 7 6 5 4 3 2

Book design by Constance Ftera
Prentice Hall Books for Young Readers
is a trademark of Simon & Schuster Inc.
Manufactured in the United States of America
Library of Congress Cataloging in Publication Data
Warren, William E., 1941-
    The headless ghost.
    Summary: Presents accounts of fifteen unexplainable
occurrences involving ghosts, poltergeists, and the
Bermuda Triangle.
    1. Curiosities and wonders—Juvenile literature.
2. Ghosts—Juvenile literature. [1. Supernatural.
2. Curiosities and wonders] I. Waldman, Neil, ill.
II. Title.
AG243.W37   1986   031'.02   85-28214
ISBN 0-13-384280-0

To Louise
with love

CONTENTS

THE HEADLESS GHOST

INTRODUCTION

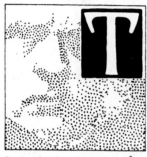

HE "TALES OF THE UNEXPLAINED" IN this book have been presented as *true* tales, for the simple reason that they have withstood the test of time; that is, they have never been disproven or shown to be anything other than true, in spite of many investigations and attempts to prove otherwise over the years.

But can we—and *should* we—believe these stories? Did they really happen? How do we know that they aren't "made up," fictional stories like James M. Barrie's *Peter Pan* or the movies "Star Wars" or "Raiders of the Lost Ark"?

Let's answer those questions with another question: How do we know that George Washington, Ben Franklin, and Thomas Jefferson actually lived? After all, none of us was alive back in the 1700s to see them, and photography, movies, and television hadn't been invented yet.

Oh, that's easy, you say: people wrote about them, and described them, and painted pictures of them, and each of them wrote so many things and did so many great things, that they *must* have lived . . .

Still, the fact remains that *none of us was there at the*

1

time. All we're doing is taking people's word that George Washington, Ben Franklin, and Thomas Jefferson were real people who lived and died, and incidentally accomplished a great deal in the process.

And, in the same way, that's precisely what we're doing in considering these tales of the unexplained. We weren't there when the Bell Witch killed off Old Jack Bell, or when the five aircraft of Flight 19 suddenly vanished into thin air as if they had never existed. We haven't confronted Anne Boleyn's headless ghost in the courtyard of the Tower of London. We've never seen Abe Lincoln's ghost sitting on the edge of his bed in the White House, calmly taking off his boots.

But because we never saw any of those things, does that mean that no one else could possibly have seen them? Or that they could *not* have happened, no matter how many people saw them?

Of course, there's a difference between these two examples. Everyone knows that Washington and Franklin and Jefferson were actual people—just as "everyone" knows that there are no such things as ghosts, and that every event has a natural, reasonable explanation, if we can only find it.

The only problem is, it doesn't always work that way. Not everything in life has a normal, ready-made, common-sense explanation. Some events are so bizarre, so unusual, that they simply defy our best efforts to explain them. As writer John B. S. Haldane put it, "The universe is not only stranger than we suppose, but stranger than we *can* suppose."

Truth *is* stranger than fiction; you've probably heard that before. And another, equally true statement is that people will believe only what they want to believe. For many people, reality consists only of what they can understand; everything else must go. Their approach to life is, if it can't be explained, it must not have happened. They aren't going to believe in ghosts until one leaps up and shouts "Boo!" in their faces.

And to make things even more complicated, there are at least four different kinds of ghost stories. First, there are fictional tales told in hushed whispers around campfires when the embers are dying and the darkness is alive with animal eyes and eerie, wailing cries in the night. You're not really supposed to believe in these stories—you're just supposed to shiver at the pictures your imagination conjures up.

A second type of ghost story is presented as a true occurrence, but when it is investigated it is found to be false. For example, escape artist Harry Houdini, himself a great believer in spiritualism, spent the latter part of his life investigating mediums (persons who claim to be able to communicate with spirits of the dead), hoping to find a medium who could reach his departed mother. He never succeeded, though, because in every case the mediums he consulted either failed completely or were found to have used gimmicks and tricks to create false impressions of such communication.

This is not to say that all seances (the meetings in which mediums try to communicate with the dead) are hoaxes or that all mediums are frauds. Houdini exposed the frauds because they *were* frauds and he was searching for the truth. But he never gave up his search as long as he lived, and he never ceased believing that there *is* a way to communicate with those who have passed on.

The third kind of ghost stories are those that have been studied and investigated thoroughly and have not been proved to be untrue despite the best efforts of experts. Literally thousands of these unexplained events and sightings have been reported, and the number grows larger with each passing year. Nearly all of the stories in this book fall into this category, which may rightly be called *true ghost stories*.

Finally, there are a small number of cases in which, while scientific investigation and psychical research is impossible for one reason or another, the stories carry the weight of truth because of the character and reliability of the witnesses involved. The first account in this book, "Ghosts in the White House," is a perfect example of this rare phenomenon.

But after all, the question of whether or not ghosts actually exist isn't really important. What *is* important is our willingness to look and decide for ourselves what we will believe, rather than merely accepting what others believe, just because they happen to believe it.

In that spirit, this book offers you a brief visit to a world you may never have explored before: it's the world of the *unexplained*, a world where nightmares as well as dreams can come true.

Famous People
Famous Ghosts

GHOSTS IN THE WHITE HOUSE

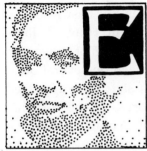 VERY YEAR, THOUSANDS OF VISI-tors to the nation's capital are led on guided tours through the magnificent white mansion at 1600 Pennsylvania Avenue in Washington, D.C. Few of those visitors are aware, though, that the White House has been home, not only to our living presidents and their families, but to a surprisingly large number of ghosts as well. And while no one has ever been permitted to conduct psychical research within the White House to investigate the many reported spectral sightings and mysterious sounds—strange, cackling laughter and anguished cries in the night, footsteps heard in empty rooms, and rappings at bedroom doors which, when opened, reveal nothing more than empty hallways—such things have occurred, and with regularity. There really *are* ghosts in the White House.

The Ghost of Abigail Adams • Construction of the White House was begun in 1792, during the term of office of George Washington. Work was still in progress eight years later when, in November of 1800, it was first occupied by our second president, John Adams, and his wife Abigail. Until that time, the nation's capital had been in New York and Philadelphia.

Living conditions in the White House were not very good when the Adamses moved in: there were no completed bathrooms, the rooms were drafty, cold, and unfinished, and no running water was available. Water had to be brought to the White House from five blocks away. Abigail Adams complained that, because no space was available for drying the family wash, she had to set up clotheslines in what is now known as the East Room.

Over a century later, during William Howard Taft's presidency (1909-1913), the ghostly figure of a woman who resembled Abigail Adams was seen on several occasions by servants and White House staff. She appeared in the East Room, wearing a long dress of the sort that was commonly worn by colonial women, and she seemed to be going through the motions of hanging clothes out to dry. At other times, the apparition was reported to have been seen in a parlor known as the Green Room, which had been a dining room when Abigail Adams lived in the White House.

The Ghost in the Garden • James Madison was the fourth president of the United States. During his second term, the nation was plunged into war with England (the War of 1812). In 1814, British troops captured Washington, D.C. and burned the White House and the Capitol, among other important buildings in the city.

Dolley Madison, the president's wife, was a popular, hard-working woman known for her talents as a hostess. In fact, with her husband out of town and the British on the march toward Washington in late August, 1814, Dolley was in the midst of preparations for an elaborate dinner party for forty guests when she received word that the city must be evacuated immediately. She managed to gather up some important government documents and a few valuables, including her parrot and the famous Gilbert Stuart painting of George Washington that is seen on our $1 bill, and fled. The next day the British took possession of the city.

Although the War of 1812 ended in December, 1814, the Madisons never again occupied the White House. They lived elsewhere during the last years of President Madison's term of office. Dolley Madison busied herself with plans for repairing and restoring the White House, including refurnishing the interior and creating beautiful gardens outside. She was especially pleased with the lovely lilacs and rose bushes that were planted during that period.

One hundred years later, Edith Wilson, the second wife of President Woodrow Wilson, decided to rearrange the rose garden that Dolley Madison had created.

Shortly after the work of transplanting was begun, the gardeners laid aside their shovels and other equipment and flatly refused to continue. They had been approached by the angry figure of a woman dressed in nineteenth-century clothing, they said. The woman demanded to know why they were making changes in her garden, and when the gardeners could not give her a satisfactory answer, she turned and stalked away angrily without leaving any footprints behind her on the dusty garden path.

Other witnesses reported seeing Dolley Madison walking in the gardens at various times of day during this period. She spoke to no one, and seemed unaware of the presence of witnesses as she slowly made her way along the paths, studying with a mixture of anger and infinite sadness the changes that were being made in her beloved gardens.

The project was quickly abandoned, and since that time no first lady has seen fit to make further changes in Dolley Madison's flower gardens.

Laughing Ghosts, Crying Ghosts • Three, and possibly four, ghosts in the White House have been identified at least partly on the basis of their laughter or crying. Frances Cleveland, wife of President Grover Cleveland, has been heard crying at night—possibly because her enormous husband (5 feet 11 inches tall, 260 pounds) was rumored to have beaten her frequently. The spectral figure of a young boy of eleven or twelve—who may be either Willie Lincoln, Abraham Lincoln's son who died at age twelve in the White House, or eleven-year-old Benjamin Pierce, who died in a train crash shortly before his father, Franklin Pierce, took office as the nation's fourteenth president—has been seen and heard running through upstairs rooms and hallways. Witnesses have had only brief glimpses of the youthful specter, but they have heard him laughing and calling out to invisible playmates as he darts from room to room.

Probably the most famous laughing ghost inhabiting the White House is Andrew Jackson, our seventh president (1829-1837). Jackson, who died at his plantation home, "The Hermitage," near Nashville, Tennessee, eight years after leaving office, is said to haunt both his home and the White House.

The Rose Room, which was President Jackson's bedroom during his terms of office, has often been described as being unaccountably chilly. And over the years, continuing up to modern times, visitors and guests have complained of hearing loud, harsh laughter in the room where Jackson slept.

In her book, *My Thirty Years Backstairs in the White House*, published in 1961, seamstress Lillian Rogers Parks reported the case of an upstairs maid who heard laughter coming from the unoccupied bed in President Jackson's bedroom. The maid, Katurah Brooks, described the laughter to Mrs. Parks as "loud" and "hollow," and said that the laughter could not have come from anywhere else but the bed. She was alone in the room at the time.

Mrs. Parks understood the maid's feelings. She herself once had felt a cold, unseen presence with her when she was working alone in the Rose Room. She left the room quickly without daring to look back. She was afraid of what she might see if she turned around.

The Ghost of Abraham Lincoln • Other ghosts have been identified in the White House, among them Presidents James A. Garfield, William McKinley, William Henry Harrison, and John F. Kennedy. But without doubt the most persistently witnessed specter in White House history has been that of Abraham Lincoln.

As most people know, President Lincoln was assassinated by actor John Wilkes Booth as Lincoln was viewing a performance at Ford's Theatre.

What is less well known is that, in life, Lincoln was a believer in psychical phenomena. At his wife's request, he participated in several seances held in the White House, at which he tried to communicate with his dead son Willie. Though his attempts did not succeed, the mediums at these seances were in agreement that Lincoln definitely had psychical powers.

One possible evidence of these "powers" may be the visions and dreams that haunted him. Once, while campaigning for the Presidency, he was preparing to rest for awhile when he happened to glance into a mirror and saw a double image of himself. One image was normal, but the other was pale and lifeless—"like a dead man's," as he explained it to his wife, Mary Todd Lincoln. Mary, who was even more inclined toward the supernatural than her husband, interpreted his vision to mean that he would be elected President twice, but that he would not live to the end of his second term of office. She was right, of course!

Less than a week before Booth's bullet put an end to his life, President Lincoln dreamed that he awoke to the sound of people crying. He rose (in his dream), went downstairs, and searched from room to room for the source of the weeping. When he arrived at the East Room, he discovered a funeral platform draped in black upon which rested a corpse wrapped in funeral garb. The face of the corpse was covered from view, and a large crowd of mourners were sobbing their hearts out in grief.

"Who is dead?" Lincoln asked of a military guard standing nearby.

"The President," the guard replied in Lincoln's dream. "He was killed by an assassin."

At that point, President Lincoln related, he woke up from his nightmare and could sleep no more that night. He had no way of knowing that, even as he related his dream to colleagues the following day, his dream would become a reality in five days' time.

Equally ominous was the fact that, on the very day of his assassination, Lincoln told his bodyguard that, for the past three nights, he had had the same dream that he would be assassinated. The bodyguard pleaded with the president to stay home that night, but Lincoln refused. He had promised his wife that they would go to the theater, he said, and besides, he was using the occasion to publicly celebrate the end of the long and bloody war.

Thus it was that Abraham Lincoln fell prey to an assassin's bullet on April 14, 1865, only five days after the Civil War was ended.

Did President Lincoln possess precognition, or the ability to see into the future through ESP (extra sensory perception)? It seems that he must have thought he had such ability, because he believed strongly in his dreams and visions. Once, while his wife Mary and son Tad were away from the White House, Lincoln wrote to warn her to watch Tad carefully because "I had an unpleasant dream about him."

Then there is the fact that Lincoln often told others of his conviction that he would not live long beyond the end of the Civil War. And as he prepared to leave for Ford's Theater with his wife on that fateful evening, he turned to his bodyguard, W. H. Crook, and said, "Goodbye." Crook thought this strange, because Lincoln had never before said *Goodbye* upon leaving for an evening engagement; he always said *Good night*.

Was this just a grisly coincidence, or a casual slip of the tongue? Or was it a hint that he actually knew, or at least suspected, what fate was waiting for him at Ford's Theater?

Like most of us, Abraham Lincoln was a man of habit, and as a politician he seldom misused words or misstated himself. He always chose his words carefully, Mr.

Crook wrote in his memoirs, so if he said *Goodbye* rather than his customary *Good night*, he must have meant it as a statement of farewell rather than one of casual parting.

It is likely that no ghost has ever appeared to as many persons in high places, whether royalty or elected government officials, as that of Abraham Lincoln. At least three presidents, two presidents' wives, and one queen have had encounters with the ghost of our sixteenth president.

Although Ulysses S. Grant, the country's eighteenth president (1869-1877), never spoke of having seen Lincoln's ghost, many of Grant's staff and White House personnel related tales of seeing or hearing Lincoln and his son Willie, especially in the corridors of the second floor, as the employees performed their White House duties. President Grover Cleveland (1885-1889) heard strange rapping sounds in the night, and President Benjamin Harrison (1889-1893) and his bodyguard were often awakened late at night by thumping sounds in Lincoln's bedroom or the hallway outside. The bodyguard reportedly attended a seance at which the ghost identified itself as that of Abraham Lincoln.

Sightings of Lincoln's ghost began with Grace Coolidge, the wife of Calvin Coolidge, our thirtieth president (1923-1929). Mrs. Coolidge saw the silhouette, or shadow, of Lincoln outlined against the backdrop of a window in the Oval Room where he often had been known to stand, deep in thought, gazing out over the countryside.

Perhaps the most famous encounter with Lincoln's ghost occurred during an official state visit to the United States in 1945 by Queen Wilhelmina of the Netherlands. While staying with President and Mrs. Franklin D.

Roosevelt at the White House, the queen was awakened one night by the sound of someone walking noisily back and forth in the hallway outside her bedroom, which was known as the Lincoln Room. It had once been the Lincolns' bedroom. As she tried to clear her mind of sleep, there came a knocking at her bedroom door. Upon opening the door, she found herself facing President Lincoln, who was dressed in a long coat and top hat.

The queen promptly fainted. When she awoke, she was lying on the floor and Lincoln was gone.

Later, when Queen Wilhelmina related her experience to President Roosevelt, he expressed little surprise. He explained that his wife Eleanor had had strange experiences when she worked late into the night. Sitting at her desk in the room that once had been Lincoln's bedroom, Mrs. Roosevelt had sometimes sensed Lincoln's presence, standing beside or behind her. Whenever she turned around, no one was there, but she still felt his presence with her. As she once said, When people live as hard as do the occupants of the White House, it is reasonable to assume that in death, their spirits would want to continue to inhabit the place where they lived.

Though Mrs. Roosevelt never actually saw or heard Lincoln's ghost, she had heard a good deal about it. Once, as she was sitting alone in her study, a maid named Mary Eban burst into the room without warning. The maid's face was wild with excitement.

"He's up there, sitting on the edge of the bed, taking off his shoes!" she cried.

"Who's up where, taking off his shoes?" the first lady asked in surprise.

"Mr. Lincoln!" the maid answered breathlessly.

Hers was not an isolated instance, either. During

FDR's long term as the nation's thirty-second president (1933-1945), there were numerous reports from White House personnel of having seen President Lincoln either sitting or lying on his bed, or standing by the same oval window where Grace Coolidge had seen him some years earlier.

Poet Carl Sandburg, who wrote a multi-volume biography of Abraham Lincoln, was another famous person to have felt, but not seen, Lincoln's presence with him in the White House. In Sandburg's case, he felt Lincoln's spirit join him as he stood by the window of the Oval Room where Lincoln so often stood in life a century before.

President Theodore Roosevelt (1901-1909) believed that Lincoln's ghost still occupied the White House. He said that he had often felt Lincoln's presence with him when he was there by himself.

Although most presidents have been reluctant to discuss their encounters with ghosts in the White House, Harry Truman (1945-1953) showed no such qualms. An outspoken, practical man, Truman saw no need to justify his belief in ghosts haunting the White House. He had experienced them, so they were there. It was as simple as that.

Truman acknowledged openly that, on several occasions, he had heard someone knocking at his door late at night, only to find no one there when he opened it. And when a visitor to the White House complained of hearing ghostly sounds in the night, Truman remarked that "It must have been Abe [Lincoln]."

Once, before a live television audience, President Truman said that he had heard a knock at his bedroom door "and answered it at about three o'clock in the morning. There wasn't anybody there. I think it must have been Lincoln's ghost walking the hall." And although he later publicly changed his mind about the sounds having been caused by a ghost, he also confessed that, on numerous occasions, he had heard similar unusual and unexplained noises.

Last Words • During President Truman's term of office, the White House was closed for extensive renovation and repair. The Trumans moved across the street to Blair House, the home of the vice presidents, until work was completed on the White House. President Truman had relatively little to say about ghosts after that, except to note at one point that he thought the presidential ghosts might still be around.

Since Harry Truman left office, no president has publicly discussed the topic, which has led some observers to conclude that the ghosts never returned to the White House after the latest renovations were completed.

Maybe.

But maybe the ghosts are still there—only no one wants to talk about them anymore. In our modern age of popularity polls, perhaps no president wants to be known as a "ghostbuster" in the White House. After all, how many votes toward re-election would any president receive if he told reporters that he hadn't been sleeping well lately because ghosts had been keeping him awake?

Yes, the ghosts are there. They aren't harmful, and they don't move things around or throw things as poltergeists have been known to do, but they're there. Every now and then an unofficial report manages to slip out; for example, Amy Carter, the daughter of Jimmy Carter, saw ghostly figures in the White House. And in 1987, President Reagan's daughter Maureen reported that she and her husband had seen a ghost in Lincoln's bedroom. They could see through it, she said; it took the form of an "outline" that ranged in color from red to deep pink.

But we don't really need such reports. Too many people of the highest character and reliability have seen the ghosts over the years for us to blame mass hysteria or other natural phenomena for the ghostly encounters.

They're there, all right—Lincoln and the rest. In a letter he wrote to his daughter Margaret in 1946, President Truman described his feelings for the White House and its ghostly inhabitants:

> This old place cracks and pops all night long and you can imagine that old [Andrew] Jackson or Andy Johnson or some other ghost is walking. Why they'd want to come back I could never understand. . . .
>
> Now about those ghosts. I'm sure they're here and I'm not half so alarmed at meeting up with them as I am at having to meet the live nuts I have to see every day. I am sure old Andy [Johnson, our seventeenth president] could give me some advice. . . And I am sure old Grover Cleveland could tell me some choice remarks to make to some political leaders. So I won't lock my doors or bar them either if any of the old coots in the pictures out in the hall want to come out of their frames for a friendly chat.

THE POLTERGEIST OF EPWORTH RECTORY

OME SUPERNATURAL HAPPENINGS must be accepted as true, not because they have been proved beyond any shadow of doubt, but because of the high moral character of the witnesses involved. Such is the case with the haunting of Epworth Rectory in Lincolnshire, England, which began in December, 1716, and ended in the latter part of January, 1717.

The poltergeist involved was named "Old Jeffery" by the children who lived at Epworth Rectory. The family was the Wesleys—the Rev. Samuel Wesley, his wife Suzannah, and nine of their children who were living at home at the time. One of those children was thirteen-year-old John Wesley, who later in life became the founder of the Methodist Church.

Although obviously a deeply religious family, the Wesleys endured nearly two months of continuous poltergeist activity that created a panic in their household and sorely tested their faith. Still, they eventually became so accustomed to the eerie groans, footsteps, creaking, rustling, squeaking, knocking, gobbling, and squealing sounds (among other things) at all hours of day and night that some of the children actually played Chase with "Old Jeffery," and followed the sounds he made as he passed from room to room.

It all began on December 1, when Nanny Marshall, one of the Wesleys' maids, reported hearing a knocking at the dining room door, followed by "several dismal groans like a person . . . at the point of death." But when she opened the door, no one was there. The Wesley family members laughed at the nanny's story and her fears—but all too soon their laughter and disbelief turned to shock.

On the following evening, Robert Brown, a servant at the rectory, was sitting with one of the maids in the dining room when both of them heard a loud knocking at the door. Mr. Brown answered the door but found no one there. As he was returning to his seat, the knocking began again, followed by the sound of someone groaning.

Thinking that the visitor was a Mr. Turpine, a family acquaintance who was ill and was known to groan frequently, the servant answered the knocking. Again no one was there. When it happened a third time, both the maid and Mr. Brown quickly decided to leave well enough alone and retire for the night.

As Brown climbed the stairs toward his bedroom on the second floor, he saw a handmill spinning by itself in the air. And after climbing into bed, he heard the sound of a turkey gobbling by his bedside, followed by the equally unsettling sound of someone stumbling over shoes, although Brown had left his shoes downstairs.

The next day, December 3, Brown and the maid related their story to another maid, who laughed at the idea of people thinking that there might be ghosts around.

"What a couple of fools you are!" she jeered. "I defy anything to frighten me!"

It wasn't long before she, too, became a believer. That same day, while she was carrying a tray full of freshly churned butter, she heard a knocking on the dairy shelf, and above it, and below it. The sound continued as she searched the shelf in vain for its source; finally, in terror, she tossed aside the tray, butter and all, and fled from the room.

On December 4, Molly—who, at twenty years old, was the eldest daughter at home—had a most frightening encounter with the ghost.

It was between five and six o'clock in the evening, and Molly was sitting alone in the study, reading. She heard the door open, but when she looked up she saw that it was still closed. Then she heard the sound of someone walking in the room, and by the rustling noise it made she could tell that it was wearing a long, silk nightgown that trailed on the floor. The noise circled completely around her, moved to the door, then apparently changed its mind and returned to circle her once more.

Then other sounds began: a knocking came from under the table; an iron casement and a warming-pan lid began to clatter; and the door latch rattled noisily up and down. Molly raced upstairs, leaped into bed still fully clothed, pulled the covers over her head, and never peeked out again till the next morning.

An evening or so later, nineteen-year-old Hetty was alone downstairs when she heard footsteps coming down an empty staircase. They proceeded past her with a thunderous tread that seemed to her to shake the house, although no one else in the house felt or heard a thing. The pounding footsteps continued down another set of stairs, and then went up two other sets of stairs before dying away into an unearthly silence.

The following day, which was either December 7 or 8 (the Wesleys' account is unclear at this point), one of the sisters—probably Emily—volunteered to inspect the rest of the house after the family retired to the upstairs bedrooms for the night. She heard a noise downstairs and followed it from the hall to the kitchen. From there she trailed it outside and back inside again. Then she heard knocking at the kitchen door. She ran to the door and jerked it open, but saw nothing. The action was repeated, but this time the door slammed against her as she stood in the open doorway. It slammed against her again as she tried to shut the door. Finally, after a brief struggle, she managed to close the door and lock it. With the knocking still ringing in her ears like the sound of someone nailing a casket shut, she went up to bed.

Next morning Mrs. Wesley, hearing of her daughter's adventure, said that she wanted to witness for herself the strange goings-on that were taking place nightly without her or her husband's knowledge. She was not entirely convinced that her children were not the culprits.

She *was* convinced from that night on, however: urged by the children to go to the nursery, she (and they) heard distinctly the sound of a cradle rocking violently back and forth in a corner of the room—*although there was no cradle in the room!*

That same evening, Emily heard a noise in the kitchen which she described as being "like a person throwing down a vast [load of] coal in the middle of the [room]." Next she heard a noise under a staircase that sounded like bottles being broken. Later, Hetty saw the figure of a man wearing a loose-fitting nightgown coming down-stairs toward her as she prepared to go to bed.

Mrs. Wesley's first impression after hearing for herself the strange sounds in the night was that they must have been caused by rats. And since the custom of the time for getting rid of rats was to blow horns loudly in order to frighten them away, that was precisely what Mrs. Wesley did.

It worked, in a way. No longer was the family both-ered by the eerie sounds only at night: from that mo-ment on, the sounds could be heard at any time of day or night!

On or about December 11, Mrs. Wesley and her youngest daughter Kezzy, who was seven years old, at-tempted to communicate with the ghost. After hearing a knocking at both ends of a bed in the nursery early that morning, Mrs. Wesley asked aloud if a spirit was present, would it answer her? She tapped her feet on the floor a number of times, and the spirit repeated the same number of knocks under her feet.

Delighted rather than frightened, young Kezzy asked if she might do likewise, and she and "Old Jeffery," as she called it, took turns knocking to each other. And when Mrs. Wesley knelt to look under the bed, she, Kezzy, and Emily saw a badger-like animal dart out from under the bed and disappear beneath Emily's petticoats. But when she lifted her skirts, there was no animal to be seen.

The disturbances continued for another ten days: there were sounds of bottles being broken, and windows clat-tering, and metal objects being tossed around, and rat-tling chains falling to the floor. All the while at odd hours were heard knocking and rapping sounds.

Strangely, though, the Rev. Mr. Wesley never heard the sounds until December 21. His wife and children were afraid to tell him what they had heard. As Mrs. Wesley wrote in a letter to her eldest son Samuel, who was living in London at the time, "We all heard it but your father, and I was not willing he should be informed of it, lest he should [think] it was against his own death, which, indeed, we all [feared]."

On the night of December 21, however, the Rev. Mr. Wesley and his wife were awakened shortly after midnight by the sound of nine very loud knocks in their bedroom. They searched the entire house, but found nothing. Throughout the next week, the minister and his wife and children continued to hear all sorts of unexplained noises such as the sounds of bouncing bumps across the floor, and of someone running up and down the stairs at night; Emily, sweeping the floors, heard the sound of unseen sweeping beside her; and her parents, searching for the source of the noises one night, clearly heard what Mrs. Wesley described as "a large pot of money [that] seemed to be poured out at my waist, and to run jingling down my nightgown to my feet." The latter was accompanied by the sound of a great many bottles breaking.

Nearly every night, "Old Jeffery" made his presence known by knocking loudly or pushing the minister during his prayers for King George's continued well-being. And on two more occasions, household members saw animals that weren't really there. Once, the animal appeared to be a badger, like the one that ran under Emily's skirts; and once, the servant Robert Brown saw and chased a white rabbit around the kitchen. The family pet, a large and powerful mastiff dog, always hid behind someone or left the room with its tail tucked meekly between its legs whenever Old Jeffery showed up.

Then, on December 28, the family heard "all the knockings as usual," as the Rev. Mr. Wesley described it, but the noises began to subside "like the rubbing of a beast against the wall," and were heard no more for nearly a month.

Old Jeffery returned to Epworth Rectory briefly between January 24-28, 1717, in the form of loud knocking noises during prayers. But in his diary for Saturday, January 29, the minister noted, "Not frightened with the continued disturbance of my family." Nor was the Wesley household ever bothered again by poltergeist activity.

This account of the haunting of Epworth Rectory is based on letters written from various family members to Samuel Wesley, and upon John Wesley's account of the haunting based on his own recollections and interviews he later conducted with everyone who had been present during the disturbances. (The interviews included the statement of a Rev. Mr. Hoole, the Vicar of Haxey, who once visited the rectory and heard the knocking sounds as they passed from room to room.)

Various Wesley family members had their own ideas of what caused the disturbances. John Wesley referred to the haunting as a "Supernatural Disturbance" in his published account in *Arminian Magazine*. His mother, Suzannah Wesley, also accepted the supernatural nature of the events, believing that it was possible to have communication "between good spirits and us." Samuel, her eldest son, held "no particular opinion concerning the events foreboded by these noises," which was hardly surprising since he was not living at home at the time.

Daughter Suzannah (Suky) Wesley believed that witch-craft was at work. She wrote to Samuel, "About a year [ago] there was a disturbance at a town near us that was undoubtedly witches, and if so near, why may they not reach us?"

Her father, on the other hand, believed it to be the work of the devil: when, during the haunting, several local clergymen and other gentlemen of the town urged him to take his family and leave the house, the Rev. Mr. Wesley replied angrily, "No, let the devil flee from me; I will never flee from the devil!"

An interesting theory about the cause of the haunting was given by Joseph Priestley, a famous scientist and the discoverer of oxygen. Years later, after studying John Wesley's article, Priestley wrote his own article for *Arminian Magazine* in which he blamed daughter Hetty for unconsciously causing the disturbances. He pointed out that, by John Wesley's account, most of the disturbances began in the nursery, or "green room," where Hetty slept.

Indeed, Mrs. Wesley noted in a letter to her son Samuel that, on one occasion, "Hetty trembled exceedingly in her sleep, as she always did before the noise awakened her. It commonly was nearer her than the rest [of the family], which she took notice of, and was much frightened, because she thought it had a particular spite at her."

Perhaps nineteen-year-old Hetty *was* the agent for Old Jeffery's poltergeist activity, since such activity is often associated with young people. Those persons around whom poltergeist disturbances are centered are known as "focus persons."

According to psychical theory, poltergeist activity often

arises as a result of emotional stresses, especially in young people, of which they may not even be aware. As these stresses build up inside the body of the focus person, sometimes the energy created transfers *outside* that person's body in a form that is powerful enough to cause poltergeist activity. And when the emotional disturbances eventually subside, the poltergeist activity disappears.

At any rate, the haunting of Epworth Rectory ranks among the most celebrated and widely-known cases of poltergeist activity on record. It is a true ghost story if ever there was one.

THE HEADLESS GHOST
OF ANNE BOLEYN

VERY YEAR ON OR ABOUT THE EVE-ning of May 19, a bizarre and ter-rifying event is said to occur in front of Blickling Hall in Norfolk, England.

From out of the darkness sur-rounding Blickling Park, a coach suddenly appears. It is drawn by a team of four black, headless horses, and driven by a headless coachman. Inside the funeral coach, a headless woman sits quietly holding her bloody head in her lap as the coach slowly makes its way along the avenue toward Blickling Hall. When the phantom coach reaches the front door, it—along with the headless specters, both animal and human—vanishes as if swallowed up by the night.

The headless apparition inside the coach is Anne Bo-leyn, second wife of King Henry VIII. Anne was Queen of England from January, 1533, until her death three years later. Her ghost returns to Blickling Hall, where she was born and spent part of her childhood, every year on the anniversary of her execution.

Anne Boleyn was beheaded on May 19, 1536.

Anne's husband, Henry VIII, was King of England from 1509 to 1547. He was a large person, as physically imposing as he was politically powerful: he stood six feet tall and weighed roughly 260 pounds.

Henry's first wife was Catherine of Aragon. Although Catherine gave birth to a daughter (Mary, who later became Queen of England), she was unable to give Henry the male heir he so keenly desired. When it finally became apparent to Henry that Catherine never was going to bear him a son to inherit the English throne, his interest in her faded and he began to look for a way out of his marriage.

Anne Boleyn was born in 1507 to wealthy, upper-class parents. Her father was Sir Thomas Boleyn, and her mother was the daughter of Thomas Howard, the second Duke of Norfolk. The Boleyn family was not exactly royalty, but they were on close speaking terms with it.

Anne spent much of her youth in France, where she served as an attendant to the French queen and grew up amid the courtly pleasures and intrigues of the French court. When she returned to England for good at about age twenty, she was a worldly young woman who knew how to handle herself among royalty. Before long, she became a maid of honor in Henry's court.

Henry quickly fell in love with Anne and began courting her in 1526, although he was still married to Catherine of Aragon at the time. Anne refused to be Henry's mistress as her sister Mary had been earlier; instead, she held out for a greater prize, namely becoming Henry's wife and Queen of England. As a result, Henry began searching for a way to divorce Catherine despite the fact that he was a Roman Catholic and divorce was forbidden by the Church.

Henry eventually obtained his divorce from Catherine after great difficulty and, on January 25, 1533, he and

Anne Boleyn were secretly married. Three months later, their marriage was publicly announced, and a month after that his divorce from Catherine of Aragon was announced. No one in England dared to question Henry's right to marry Anne before he was officially divorced from Catherine.

In September of 1533, Anne gave birth to a daughter, Elizabeth (who later, as Queen Elizabeth I, would become England's greatest queen). Henry was royally disappointed in his young bride for not bearing him a son. He began to lose interest in Anne at that point, and turned away from her as he had done earlier with his first wife.

When Anne later suffered the loss of two children, in 1534 and 1536, without having borne Henry a son who lived, her fate was sealed. She was brought to trial on charges of treason, witchcraft, and extreme unfaithfulness to her husband. At her trial, she was quickly and unanimously convicted, sentenced to death, and sent to the Tower of London to await execution.

She had been abandoned by virtually everyone in her life: even her own father had proclaimed her guilt publicly out of fear of Henry's wrath, and her uncle, an official at her trial, had imposed the death penalty on her.

Throughout her imprisonment, Anne continued to protest her innocence of all charges, and carried herself with a dignity and courage befitting a queen. Even on the scaffold, kneeling before the chopping block, she was able to joke with the executioner about his ability to complete the job on her tiny neck in one stroke.

After the foul deed was done on the morning of May 19, 1536, Henry was free to marry again. But England was not freed from the memory—or the ghost—of Anne Boleyn.

According to one theory, ghosts are the spirits of people who have died, usually violently or suddenly. They either do not understand, or refuse to accept, that they are no longer alive. Thus, rather than passing on to after-death existence in some other dimensional plane, their spirits remain earthbound, lingering in the areas they were familiar with in life and appearing in spectral form from time to time by means that we do not understand.

Anne Boleyn's death was both violent and sudden. After her execution, Henry refused to let her receive a proper Christian family burial among her ancestors on Boleyn property as was the custom of the times; instead, he ordered that Anne be buried without any sort of religious ceremony in a small church within the Tower itself. It was widely rumored—but never proven—that her body was secretly removed from its Tower grave in the dead of night and taken to Sale, where it was reburied beneath an unmarked, black slab.

Anne's headless ghost has appeared, not only in Norfolk where she was born, but at two other residences of her youth: Rochford Hall in Essex, where Anne spent part of her childhood; and Hever Castle in Kent, where Henry first courted her in 1526.

However, the most famous site to be haunted by her restless, wandering spirit has been the Tower of London, where she was imprisoned and executed in 1536. A nineteenth-century officer of the guard reportedly saw her one night in royal garb, and with her head intact, leading a ghostly procession within the chapel of St. Peter-ad-Vincula, the small church in the Tower of London where Anne supposedly was buried.

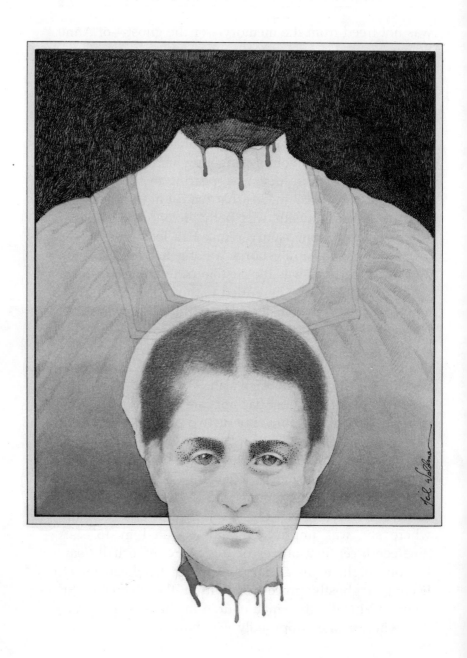

Anne's headless form has been seen on several occasions in the White Tower, the oldest part of the Tower of London. Two sightings in particular have helped to make her the most famous ghost in English history.

In 1864, a Tower guard who was on trial for falling asleep on duty testified at his court-martial that he had not been sleeping when he was found lying unconscious; instead, he claimed that he had fainted in terror after encountering the headless figure of a woman dressed in white.

The sentry explained to the court that he had been standing in the sentry box near the Lieutenant's Lodgings on the night in question when a figure clad in white suddenly appeared before him. He challenged the figure with the familiar "Who goes there?" It gave no response, but moved closer to him until, in desperation, he ran the figure through with a forward thrust of the bayonet at the end of his rifle.

"What happened then?" he was asked.

The sentry explained that, when he jabbed through the figure with his bayonet, "a fiery flash ran up the bayonet and scorched my hand."

At that point, he said, he dropped the rifle—and could not recall what happened from that time until the corporal of the guard who was sent out to relieve him a few minutes later found him lying unconscious in the snow.

The sentry was asked if he could remember enough to describe the appearance of the figure in white. He said that he could.

"It was the figure of a woman wearing a queer-looking bonnet—but there wasn't no head inside the bonnet!"

Quite naturally, the officers of the court considered the

sentry's story too fantastic to be true. But their disbelief soon turned to shock as a parade of witnesses testified that they, too, had seen the headless woman in the Tower that same evening. The court listened in stunned silence as an officer testified under oath that he had not only seen the woman that night, but he also had heard the guard challenge her presence by crying out, "Who goes there?," and he had watched in horror as the guard thrust his bayonet through the ghostly figure in white with no apparent effect. The woman simply walked through the bayonet, the rifle, and the guard as well, the officer continued, at which time the guard fainted and the woman disappeared. The officer's testimony matched that of the guard and other witnesses in every detail.

Eventually, the sentry was declared not guilty. And while the court's verdict of innocence does not prove that the events of that terrible evening actually took place exactly as described, it lends credibility to the widely held belief that the headless ghost of Anne Boleyn is more than the product of someone's hysteria or overactive imagination.

Multiple-witness cases, or those in which a number of spectators are present during a ghostly encounter, are relatively rare. They are an extremely valuable tool to psychical researchers in two important respects. First, there is the additional weight of evidence provided by the presence of several witnesses, who are more likely to be believed than a single observer who might otherwise be accused of hallucinating, or "seeing things." Second, when the witnesses are able to agree on even the slightest details of the sighting—as was the case in the 1864 Tower of London sighting of Anne Boleyn's ghost—mass hysteria can be ruled out as a possible explanation for the ghostly encounter.

A sighting that was strikingly similar to the 1864 encounter occurred in the Tower in 1933. As before, the sentry on duty challenged the headless figure, and again the woman passed through the startled sentry's bayonet and rifle. Terrified, the sentry dropped his rifle and fled, screaming. No other witnesses were present on this occasion, but the guard could not be swayed from his story.

Since most of the sightings of this headless ghost have involved one witness and single occurrences, they cannot be said to possess any great degree of believability in themselves; still, when added to the larger body of sightings of Anne Boleyn which have occurred over the years since her death (including the remarkable multiple-witness sighting of 1864), they present a far more compelling case for the likelihood that her spirit still resides in England and appears in ghostly, headless form from time to time.

But Anne Boleyn is not the only wife of Henry VIII whose ghost has been seen!

On May 30, 1536, eleven days after Anne Boleyn was led up the wooden scaffold staircase to meet her fate on the executioner's chopping block, Henry VIII remarried. It was his third marriage, his bride's first. She was a rather plain, frail young girl named Jane Seymour.

Although married to Henry for only one year before she died in childbirth in 1537, Jane Seymour would remain Henry's favorite among his six wives, and for a very special reason: she was the only one to bear him a surviving male child as he so greatly desired.

Jane Seymour's ghostly apparition has been seen time

and again—even in modern times—in the Silver Stick Gallery at Hampton Court Palace, carrying a long, tapering candle as she glides soundlessly up or down the staircase and across the Gallery. It has been suggested that her spirit is searching for the ghost of Anne Boleyn, whose death allowed Jane to become the third wife of Henry VIII. Possibly she felt guilty about having played a part, however innocently, in bringing about Anne's death.

Henry's fourth wife was the German princess Anne of Cleves, whom he married in 1540 for political reasons rather than for love. In truth, he hated the very sight of her, and divorced her in 1541. Eighteen days later, he married Catherine Howard, a beautiful twenty-year-old cousin of the unfortunate Anne Boleyn.

By this time, Henry was 49 years old, grossly overweight, and suffering from a variety of illnesses that would end his life seven years later. His condition took a severe turn for the worse when his aides brought him undeniable evidence that his young wife was being unfaithful to him.

Thus it was that, on February 13, 1542, after only eighteen months of marriage to the king, Catherine Howard was beheaded in the Tower of London, along with all of her former lovers.

Today, the shrieking, screaming ghost of Catherine Howard haunts Hampton Court Palace, rushing frantically along the "Haunted Gallery" that leads to the chapel, pursued by a host of ghostly soldiers. Apparently, her spirit is reenacting one of the final scenes of her life: as she was being led away for imprisonment and later execution in the Tower, she broke loose from the guards who were accompanying her and raced across the gallery, trying in vain to reach Henry, who was praying for her in the Hampton Court Palace chapel.

Her ghost has also been seen in more placid surroundings: in the gardens of Hampton Court, and in Eythorn Manor, Hollingbourne, Kent. At such times she is calm and composed, and appears to be enjoying a leisurely daytime stroll through the gardens, as she often did in life before she met and married Henry and later lost her head.

It is interesting to note, too, that although the ghosts of three of Henry's six wives—Anne Boleyn, Jane Seymour, and Catherine Howard—have been seen on numerous occasions, and in various locations in England, no one has ever reported seeing Henry's ghost. You might think that, after divorcing two of his wives and having two others beheaded, Henry might have felt guilty or uneasy enough to produce a restless ghost of his own after he died—but he didn't. As far as anyone knows, Henry's spirit was laid to rest peacefully when he was buried in Westminster Abbey in 1547.

Haunted Places

THE HAUNTING OF BALLECHIN HOUSE

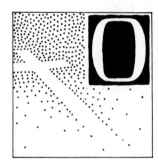NE OF THE GREATEST PROBLEMS OF psychical research, at least where hauntings are concerned, is the tendency of individual occurrences to be relatively brief. As occult expert David Knight explained in his introduction to *Best True Ghost Stories of the 20th Century*,

Unless a researcher is on the spot when the events begin, or shortly afterward, his opportunity is gone. And sometimes the activity ceases completely in the presence of strangers or when the focus person or persons [the one(s) around whom the disturbance is centered] leave the scene. Moreover, the disturbances usually end as abruptly and unexpectedly as they start.

When parapsychologists—psychical researchers—have arrived in time to study hauntings in progress, however, the results sometimes have been spectacular.

In 1898, a team of dedicated psychical researchers studied a haunted house in the Scottish Highlands at Logierait, Perthshire, during the period of its haunting. The mansion was Ballechin House, home of the Stewart family since 1806.

Actually, the story begins with an article that appeared in the London *Times* in June, 1897. It described the supernatural terrors encountered by an anonymous family which had taken a year's lease on Ballechin House and its huge estate in the autumn of 1896. The family left the house for good with more than ten months left on their twelve-month lease—which was already paid in full—after hearing ghostly, limping footsteps in a bedroom, seeing ghosts who faded away or walked through walls, and waking night after night in a cold sweat to the sounds of blood-curdling screams, moaning, or heavy pounding on their bedroom doors at night, only to find no one there.

The *Times* article was noted with interest by various members of Britain's Society for Psychical Research (S.P.R.), some of whom already were aware of the ghostly goings-on at Ballechin House. Now that the occupants were gone and the house was available, a group of S.P.R. members decided to rent Ballechin House for the purpose of conducting psychical research.

When they began, the five S.P.R. members who participated in the project were not trying either to prove or to disprove the existence of ghosts, apparitions, or poltergeists in Ballechin House. All they intended to do was to live in the house continuously for one year and see for themselves what truth, if any, there was to the stories they had read and heard about.

They were not disappointed: in all, they recorded 116 separate instances of unexplained sounds alone during their stay at Ballechin House—and that figure does not include the many spectral sightings, or the strange *smells* that were noted, or the instances of someone's being touched when no one was there.

In describing the sounds they heard, they used such terms as "loud clanging sounds in the room," "groans," "explosive noises," "crash under dome," "metallic clangs," "movements of (unseen) animals in the room," "vibrating bangs," "voices and footsteps in room overhead (empty)," "heavy blow on table," "shuffling of slippered feet," "violent hammering on door in daylight," "voices of a man and woman arguing," and "the sound of someone reading aloud."

Additionally, two witnesses once saw the stooped, crippled figure of a ghostly hunchback gliding upstairs; several people insisted that they heard the sounds of panting dogs beating their wagging tails against doors; and a stunned guest said that he had seen a ghostly hand holding a crucifix floating in the air at the foot of his bed. The hand was not attached to anything at all.

The year-long investigation was financed entirely by one of the Society's well-to-do members who volunteered to pay all expenses. This was no small undertaking, either, considering that: (a) it was necessary to rent the entire 4,400-acre estate, and not merely the house; (b) the house was unfurnished, empty, dirty, and cold, and had to be cleaned and equipped with furniture, food, fuel, and other supplies in order to make the place livable; (c) a full-time household staff, including maids, cooks, and other servants had to be hired; and (d) at any given time during the investigation, a large number of guests was likely to be found at Ballechin House. These guests were "selected volunteers" who were known to be familiar with psychic research, or who were at least sympathetic to the subject. They acted as unpaid observers who reported what they experienced.

In order for their findings to be as accurate as possible,

the researchers kept detailed records of every sighting, including the time of day or night when observed, the length of the encounter, who was present, and precise descriptions of what each witness saw, heard, felt, or even smelled. After encounters were over, the witnesses sat together and compared impressions, trying to determine the extent to which the sounds, visions, etc., had been the same for each witness.

Once a given room had been the site of a haunting episode, the researchers would swap duty watch in that room to permit others to compare the sensations they experienced with those that had been experienced previously. They were nothing if not thorough researchers.

In addition to conducting interviews with everyone in the area who had lived or served at Ballechin and had firsthand knowledge of its previous hauntings, the researchers attempted to communicate with the house's haunting spirits. Two spirits identified themselves as *Ishbel* and *Margharaed*, which were Irish for *Isabel* and *Margaret*. Isabella was a sister of the Major Robert Stewart whose death in 1876 apparently triggered the hauntings; and Margaret presumably was a nun who, like Isabella, lived at a nun's retreat that was located on the estate.

The disturbances observed during this time may be grouped into three major categories: those involving religious figures, such as nuns or priests; those involving the figure that was heard limping around one of the beds; and the eerie problems that arose concerning dogs in Ballechin House.

Nuns and Priests • From the very first, investigators, guests, and servants reported hearing noises that sounded like a priest chanting or reading aloud, presum-

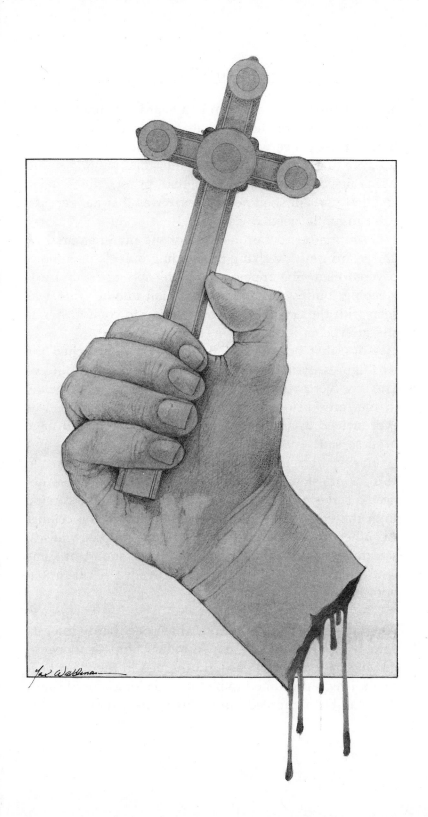

ably in Latin. A servant who had heard the chanting told researchers before she left that, according to local tradition, a priest once was murdered at Ballechin House by the wife of a former owner. Whether this chanting sound was caused by the ghost of that priest, the woman couldn't say. All she knew for sure was that her services were urgently needed elsewhere!

On numerous occasions, one of the investigators saw and heard a nun walking or standing outside in a snow-covered glen. She appeared to be terribly upset and was weeping loudly. On another occasion another nun was seen with the crying sister, attempting to comfort her as she grieved in loud, heaving sobs.

A dog that belonged to the observer approached the two figures, barking furiously, but they paid it no heed. The observer noticed that the only footprints in the snow in that area belonged to the dog. No explanation was ever arrived at as to why the spectral nun should have been so sad.

Shortly after the death of Major Robert Stewart in 1876, a priest who was staying at Ballechin House noticed a series of strange noises that seemed to be coming from the empty space between his bed and the ceiling. At other times he also heard loud rapping noises, screaming, and the distinctly unsettling sound of some kind of large animal hurling itself against his bedroom door in the night.

The Limping Figure • More than one hardy investigator was unnerved by the sound of limping footsteps moving back and forth around the bed in the main bedroom. It was presumed to be the ghost of Major Stewart, who had been crippled during his military days in India.

The room in which he prowled, limping, at night had once been the bedroom of his housekeeper, Sarah. In fact, she had died in that room, which the investigators later described as the most haunted room in Ballechin House.

The Man Who Wanted to Become a Dog • Easily the weirdest part of the haunting of Ballechin House was the relationship between Major Stewart and his fourteen dogs. He not only loved them, but he actually preferred their company to that of humans. He often told others that, after he died, he expected his spirit to live on in the body of his favorite dog, a black spaniel.

When the major died in 1876 at age seventy, his relatives quickly had all of his dogs rounded up and shot to death—including the black spaniel. Apparently, they didn't want to take chances, however slight, that the major's spirit might reveal itself through the dog and disinherit someone. Major Stewart, being unmarried, had no direct heirs; thus, according to his will, his entire estate went to his married sister's eldest surviving son.

Some years later, that son's wife was at work in the study one day when she began to notice an aroma she hadn't smelled in that room since before the major died: the unmistakable odor of *dogs*. She looked around to assure herself that she was alone, then suddenly leaped and gave a small cry of fright: as she told her husband excitedly a short while later, she felt herself being pushed by what felt like an invisible dog.

Possibly the most frightening experience of the entire investigation involved dogs. It occurred one night early in May, 1898. The observer, Miss Adela Goodrich-Freer, was asleep in bed with her pet dog when she was awakened by the dog's frantic whimpering. She hastily lit a candle and glanced around the room, only to find a pair of black dog's paws lying on her bedside table. She thought about waking her roommate to find out if she, too, could see the paws. But even as she was trying to decide what to do, the paws faded and disappeared from view.

The Alleged Haunting of B------ House • The investigation and research ended when the year's lease expired in February, 1899. Later that year, Miss Goodrich-Freer and Lord Bute (the member of the Society for Psychical Research who had paid all expenses for the investigation) co-authored a book in which they described in great detail their psychical experiences and investigation of the haunting at Ballechin House.

Unfortunately, knowing in advance that the Stewarts were strongly opposed to making public such intimate family secrets, the authors decided to omit all references to the owners' names, including the name of the house. Thus, the title of the book was *The Alleged Haunting of B------ House.* It was first published in 1899, and appeared again in 1900, but it never made any kind of serious impact on the reading public, probably because of the silly title and omission of proper names.

It wasn't an "alleged" haunting; it was a *real* haunting, at least in the mind of every person who took part in the investigation or spent time in Ballechin House during the investigation.

It wasn't an "alleged" haunting to the maid who awakened one morning to find herself facing the figure of a woman whose upper body, wrapped in a shawl, was floating beside her bed. The woman had no lower body at all. And it wasn't an "alleged" haunting to a guest who was awakened by a pair of unseen hands that were trying to tear off his nightshirt and pajamas.

But the public simply wasn't interested in an "alleged" haunting that happened to unnamed persons in an unknown house; instead, readers wanted names, dates, and locations—all of which the authors had in abundance, but decided not to use. And that was a shame: if the true story of the haunting of Ballechin House had gotten out—including the excellent investigation conducted by members of the S.P.R.—it would have found a wide audience and would have convinced scoffers that ghost stories can be true.

THE COONIAN
DEVIL-GHOST

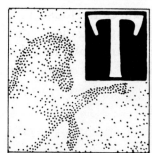HE WORD *POLTERGEIST* IS GERMAN for "noisy ghost." Poltergeists are never seen; instead, they make their presence known by the sounds they make, such as laughing, talking, groaning, crying out, rapping on doors or walls, or ringing bells, or else by moving or throwing objects, touching people, or the like. For this reason, they are often referred to as "mischievous spirits."

Generally, poltergeist activities or disturbances are more or less benign; that is, while they may be bothersome, or even frightening in some cases, people are seldom harmed by them.

Sometimes, though, poltergeist hauntings can be both frightening *and* dangerous.

In Coonian, Ireland, an intelligent poltergeist amused itself by playing an assortment of rather harmless tricks on a family, and then left a lasting, bitter impression on three priests who were sent to the haunted house by their bishop to perform an exorcism.

The house in question had been up for sale several times: it was rumored that an old pensioner had once been robbed and murdered there on the day he received his monthly check. Since then, a parade of owners had bought, and quickly sold, the house without an explanation beyond vague references to unearthly goings-on. In fact, one owner stayed just one night before moving his family out and offering the house for sale again.

By the time the Murphys—Mrs. Murphy and her six children, who ranged in age from nine years old to twenty-five—moved into the house, the disturbances were occurring regularly: pillows snatched from under sleeping heads; sounds of snoring in the dark, and human shapes seen beneath the sheets in empty beds; bedcovers pulled off family members and tossed across the room; lights going out suddenly and mysteriously; the sensation and sound of something unseen rushing either down from, or up toward, the ceiling; and other weird sounds like the kicking of a horse, or hissing, or whistling, or an invisible dog lapping at invisible water.

Soon the local bishop was consulted about the Thing— whatever it was—that was upsetting and disturbing the Murphys' home life. The bishop, in turn, sent out three priests at different times, separately or in pairs, to investigate the disturbances.

One priest who, in the course of fifty visits to the house, became familiar enough with the poltergeist to refer to it as "Johnny," told of a night visit he had made to the house. When he arrived, Mrs. Murphy and two of her young daughters were sleeping in the living room on pallets set near the hearth. A fire was blazing in the fireplace. He asked the children why they were not in bed, and they indicated that bad things were going on in their bedroom.

Finally, the priest was able to persuade the youngsters to return to bed by promising to accompany them and

tuck them in for the night. No sooner were they in bed, however, than a sound arose like that of a neighing, wildly bucking horse. The bedcovers were ripped off the bed and hurled aside.

Thinking that surely the children themselves must be responsible for this trickery, the priest gathered their hands together and held them down with one of his own, and laid his other hand over their feet as well, but the disturbance continued as violently as before.

The priest, now aware that the children were not causing it, suggested aloud that perhaps the Devil was the unseen force in the room. He challenged it to show itself.

Instantly, a loud hiss was heard by all three humans in the room. A shape like a large rat was seen moving around under the bedcovers, and the priest felt something that he later described as the feeling of an *eel* twisting itself around his wrist.

At other times, the poltergeist appeared to be in a playful mood; sometimes it seemed intent on showing its spellbound witnesses how intelligent it was.

For example, a priest who visited the house sixteen times once heard a musical sound coming from the ceiling. Speaking to the poltergeist, he suggested that perhaps it might like to whistle for them, which is precisely what it did.

The priest also stated that, using rapping sounds for answers, the spirit was able to answer correctly questions put to it in Irish and in Latin—questions such as "How many of us were born in Ireland?" and "How many of us were born in County Monaghan?" The answers were correctly given even when guests who were previously unknown to the Murphys were present, which ruled out the possibility that any of the family knew the answers beforehand. Besides, of those present, only the priest understood Latin, so even if anyone knew the answers, he couldn't understand the questions when the priest spoke in Latin.

Sometimes the poltergeist playfully tapped out the

tune to "The Soldier's Song" on request; and, when sprinkled with holy water on one occasion, it angrily played the tune "Boyne Water."

On a different occasion, after listening to outsiders' accusations that the children were to blame for the mysterious noises heard by all who entered the house, another priest decided to duplicate the earlier experiment with the children in bed. When a loud knocking commenced around the youngsters' bed, the priest told two of the witnesses in the room to hold the children's hands and feet firmly in place, which they did as the priest sat on the edge of the bed.

After about ten minutes in which the knocking sound continued without letup, the two men suddenly leaped up at the same time. Wide-eyed, they both said that some invisible Thing had begun punching at them and pushing them off the bed. They absolutely refused to sit down on it again.

The priest, too, felt the presence of the unseen spirit-force. It did not push or punch at him, but he felt something moving behind him, up and down the length of the bed.

Probably the most frightening occurrence to take place while the Murphy family inhabited the house arose when a priest and one of the Murphy sons—James, aged twenty-five—witnessed someone's death in one of the bedrooms. In an otherwise empty bed, they saw bed-clothes suddenly begin to assume the shape of a human form inside them, thrashing and heaving rapidly in the chest area as if someone were struggling to breathe.

James Murphy and the priest hurried to the kitchen where the rest of the family and another priest were gathered. The entire group returned with them to the bedroom to watch the unearthly scene.

The body-less shape inside the bedclothes was lying diagonally across the bed, and its movements were even more frenzied and erratic than before. The witnesses clearly heard heavy, labored breathing and a rattling, gurgling sound from deep in the "person's" throat. The priest described it as resembling "what country people would call a 'hard death'."

Finally, after about ten minutes of vigorous struggling and gasping breaths by the shape in the bed, the movements and sounds died away. The room grew deathly silent, and the bedclothes slowly lost their shape and became just that: bedclothes, lying on an empty bed.

The dates of the Coonian haunting (1913-1914) are the years when the priests were associated with the house while the Murphys were living there. In 1914, the Murphys moved out and sailed off to a new home in the United States. And that was the end of the haunting, as far as they were concerned.

In a fictional ghost story, this would be the point where the storyteller slowly closes his book, looks up at his eager listeners, and smiles gently as he utters the familiar line, "And they all lived happily ever after."

But this isn't a fictional ghost story. The house is a real house in Coonian, Ireland; the Murphys were real people; the priests who were sent to the house to exorcise (or *cast out*) any demons within it were real priests; and the Thing—whether a ghost, or poltergeist, or devilish demon—was all too real. Of the three priests who were sent to investigate the haunting, one contracted spinal meningitis, another suffered facial paralysis, and the third had a nervous breakdown.

THE DEVIL'S
TRAMPING GROUND

OR MORE THAN 150 YEARS, THE LEGend has persisted that the Devil himself takes nightly walks in North Carolina. The spot, known familiarly as the Devil's Tramping Ground, is said to be where the Devil paces in a circle every night as he meditates upon new ways to cause trouble and suffering for humanity.

That much is legend; the truth is that no vegetation, whether trees, or flowers, or grass, or even weeds (except for minute amounts of a tall, slender, weedlike grass called wire grass), has ever been known to grow within the circular clearing in the woods. For at least as long as man has inhabited the area, this circle has been barren and lifeless, for reasons that defy any kind of logical analysis.

The Devil's Tramping Ground is located ten miles west of Siler City, one mile from Harper Cross Roads in Warren County, North Carolina. There, just off the road in a lightly forested area on land that is privately owned, it is surrounded by pine trees, both thick and slender, and by towering oak trees and underbrush.

In contrast to the abundant plant life around it, though, the well-worn clearing is as barren as the surface of the moon. It measures exactly forty feet in diameter, and is perfectly round as if unknown surveyors had measured it before clearing away all plant life.

A narrow path no more than a foot or two wide forms the outer boundary of the clearing. One theory has it that the clearing was created by the hoofs of horses and mules as they walked in a continuous, circular path, supplying "horsepower" for a mill that once stood on the spot to grind sugar cane into cane syrup.

Certainly the constant motion of horses walking the same circular route, hour after hour, day after day, would have killed off all vegetation along the outer "path." And it is equally true that there were—and are, even today—cane-grinding operations in the area. But the clearings of other abandoned sugar cane mills nearby have all been overgrown with underbrush and trees over the years since they were last used, while the Devil's Tramping Ground remains unaccountably free of plant life.

Two shallow holes mark the center of the clearing. They were made by unknown vandals or treasure-hunters who apparently decided that the spot must have been the location of buried treasure.

Between the holes and the outer path, the rocky soil looks as if someone—or *something*—had recently raked it smooth. Indeed, local people will tell you that, on countless occasions, they or other visitors to the site have left sticks, stones, or other objects inside the clearing overnight, only to return early next morning to find the objects gone and the clearing looking as if it had been freshly swept.

Outside the clearing, grass and weeds grow to the very edge of the path—but not inside it. Nothing grows

inside the clearing, except the suspicion that something unearthly is at work here.

It is only natural that, over the years, people have attempted to explain in both natural and supernatural terms the lingering presence of the strange clearing that won't go away, in the woods near the center of North Carolina.

The most popular theory is that the Devil's Tramping Ground was once an Indian gathering place. At this spot, the legend goes, Indian tribes often came together in large numbers to celebrate certain occasions with feasting or dancing, to observe religious ceremonies, or to hold war councils. In each case, there would have been vigorous activities performed, such as ceremonial or war dances. And over the years, as hundreds and thousands of moccasined feet danced to the accompaniment of Indian drums, the earth beneath their feet would have grown bare and lifeless. Some Indians say their Great Spirit keeps the clearing as it was in former times, as a testament to the faith of those warriors. Others say that the clearing holds the earthly remains of a great Indian chieftain who was slain in battle and buried there.

Another theory (which has never been thoroughly investigated) holds that the clearing is the result of high salt content in the soil. Salt has been found in the soil in many locations in central and eastern North Carolina; and since salty soil tends to discourage the growth of most plants, this is one possible reason for the lack of plants within the clearing.

Closely allied to this theory is another which has more basis in fact: when agents of the North Carolina State Department of Agriculture tested soil taken from the

Devil's Tramping Ground, their tests showed that the soil completely lacked any of the nutrients necessary for plant growth. Why this should be so, in this particular spot and in no other in the state, they had no earthly idea.

Equally mysterious is the problem of why the soil should be either salty *or* sterile in a perfectly circular shape.

Perfect circles are virtually unheard of in nature. The earth is not perfectly round, nor does the moon's orbit around the earth follow a perfect circle. Water droplets are not perfectly round, since the pull of gravity affects their shape. Why, then, should a single forty-foot circular patch of ground in North Carolina be any different from the soil just inches outside the circle?

Even if the soil *is* barren, as the state's tests proved, why hasn't the soil of the Devil's Tramping Ground built itself up over the hundreds of years since the clearing has been known to exist? Virtually everywhere on earth, soil is constantly changing through the addition of many sources of nutrients: those carried in tiny quantities by the wind and rain, or added by decaying matter or by insect activity. Yet the Devil's Tramping Ground remains lifeless except for a few straggly strands of wire grass.

Perhaps it *is*, as locals say, the work of the Devil himself. No one knows for sure, though, because no one is known ever to have spent the night there, waiting for the Devil to appear after night has fallen and darkness has descended upon the earth.

THE SECRET OF
GLAMIS CASTLE

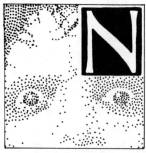N O BOOK OF TALES OF THE SUPER-
natural would be complete with-
out a story about a haunted castle.

This is the story of the most famous haunted castle of all: Glamis
Castle, in County Angus, Scotland. Somewhere within this castle lies a secret room, whose
location is unknown except to certain family members.
And within the room is said to reside a Horror that is so
terrible, and so frightening, that merely to look upon it
would drive you mad.

Actually, Glamis Castle would be famous even if it did
not possess such a bizarre secret. It is the family home of
England's Queen Mother—the mother of Queen Elizabeth II—and it was at Glamis that Princess Margaret was
born.

Glamis Castle is nearly six hundred years old. It was
built sometime in the late 1300s, toward the end of the
Middle Ages. Its owners—the ancient Lords of Glamis
and present-day Earls of Strathmore, all members of the
Bowes-Lyons family—have lived there continuously ever
since.

The castle was so well known even in the 1500s that
William Shakespeare made Glamis the location of one of
his most famous plays, the tragedy *Macbeth*. (In his play,

Macbeth was the thane, or clan chieftain, of Glamis who murdered Duncan II, the Scottish king.) And while the historical events portrayed in *Macbeth* occurred some 350 years before Glamis Castle was built, it is easy to see why Shakespeare chose Glamis as the setting for his play: with its tall, gray, fortified stone walls and abundant towers and turrets, Glamis looks like nothing so much as a great, gray beast crouched and lying in wait in the valley beneath Hunter's Hill, where another Scottish king, Malcolm II, was murdered in the year 1034.

Inside, the ancient castle is hardly less gloomy and cheerless: some of its more than one hundred rooms have been carved out of stone walls that measure fifteen feet thick in places; they are connected by a maze-like series of long, cold corridors and passageways of stone, and broad staircases that have seen their share of misfortune, terror, and tragedy over the years.

And over everything hangs the dark cloud of *the mystery*: the closely-guarded family secret, so terrible that only three people alive know its answer—the present Earl of Strathmore, his steward, and his eldest son, who traditionally is told the nature of the secret on the evening of his twenty-first birthday.

No one else on earth—not the earl's wife, nor his daughters or other sons, nor his closest friends—has ever found out or been told the secret. It is one of the most enduring, closely-guarded secrets on earth.

Unquestionably, the secret involves horrors held sacred by those who know it. In the early 1900s, the man who was then Earl of Strathmore told a questioner, "If you could guess the nature of this secret, you would go down on your knees and thank God it were not yours." And although on several occasions young heirs have vowed to reveal the secret after it is passed on to them, none has ever done so. It is said that, having learned the nature of the Horror, they are so overwhelmed by it that their lives are never again the same.

Outsiders have tried to discover the secret for themselves. In the most famous attempt, a group of houseguests at Glamis in the late 1800s took advantage of the

earl's temporary absence to search for the hidden room. Basing their search on the notion that the room must have had a window, they went around the house draping towels from the windows of every room they found. Later, when they finished their task, they went outside to find that several windows had no towels in them— which meant that several rooms could not be reached by conventional doorways.

Before they could complete their search, however, the earl returned and angrily ordered the guests to leave the premises.

What is the nature of this terrible secret or curse that haunts Glamis Castle and fascinates outsiders to the extent that Glamis has been called "the most famous haunted house in England"? Are there any clues at all as to what sort of nameless Horror might be found in the missing room?

Many theories have been offered over the years; some of them are more fantastic than others. None of them may in fact be true. Or, on the other hand, perhaps *all* of them are true . . .

The Legend of Earl Beardie • Around 1450, the Lord of Glamis Gastle was a wild-tempered man whose thick beard earned him the local nickname (unknown to him, of course), of "Earl Beardie." He was a loud, vulgar person whose favorite joy in life was gambling, especially playing cards.

One Sunday night in November, the earl decided to find someone at Glamis to play cards with. Aware of the coarse language and violent temper he displayed when gambling, each person he invited to play politely begged off, giving one excuse or another. The women of the castle, the servants, and even the chaplain all had something else to do. Finally, in disgust, Earl Beardie stormed off to his room, vowing that he would be willing to play even with the Devil himself.

Soon there came a knocking at his bedroom door. A stranger appeared, asking if the earl still wanted a gambling partner. In practically no time, they were involved in a game so tense and loud that their oaths and shouting could be heard all over the huge castle.

One servant, overcome by curiosity, crept up to the door and peeked through the keyhole. No sooner had he done so, however, than the stranger shouted, "Smite that eye!" He pointed a long, bony finger at the keyhole, whereupon a shaft of incredibly bright light appeared and shot toward the keyhole. Blinded and screaming in pain, the servant staggered backward and collapsed on the floor. Earl Beardie quickly saw to the servant's injury, but when he turned back to the room the stranger was gone.

As you probably have guessed by now, the stranger in the legend was none other than the Devil himself. And because the Devil played for, and won, Earl Beardie's soul—or so it was said—every Sunday evening in November after the earl died, the castle resounded with the gamblers' cries as they continued their unearthly game with shouts and oaths and quarreling.

Finally, when the residents of Glamis could endure no more, they bricked up the room and left Earl Beardie to his fate: playing cards with the Devil until the end of time.

The Witch of Glamis • Beautiful Janet Douglas, the Lady Glamis, was the wife of the sixth Laird (Lord) of Glamis in the 1500s. When her husband was found poisoned to death one morning, Lady Glamis was accused of murdering him. She was tried for the crime, but she was acquitted for lack of evidence.

A few years later, though, her luck ran out: this time she was charged with conspiring to murder Scotland's king, James V, and also accused of being a witch. She was quickly tried, convicted on false testimony, and burned at the stake in the year 1537.

Some people say the secret of Glamis Castle is that, somewhere in a hidden dungeon or bricked-up room, the witch is trapped and trying to get out. Her unearthly shrieks and cries can sometimes still be heard in the night as she restlessly prowls her prison of cold unyielding stone.

The Skeletons in the Dungeon • Sometime during the 1600s, two local clans were engaged in a bitter, bloody feud. One day, sixteen members of the Ogilvie clan arrived breathlessly at Glamis Castle, pleading for protection from a band of Lindsays who were chasing them.

Although the Laird of Glamis was not involved in the feud, he took them in. Instead of showing his weary, frightened guests to comfortable quarters for the night, however, he led them to a secret chamber, locked them in, and left them to starve to death.

For many years after their deaths, residents of Glamis Castle could hear shouts and groans coming from somewhere deep within the castle. Finally, an Earl of Strathmore decided to investigate. He followed the sounds until he came to their source, a little-known locked room which he had never entered before. Upon entering the room, he took one look around, staggered backward, and fainted into the arms of his faithful steward.

Afterward, he refused to discuss what he had seen, and he quickly had the room bricked up so that no one else might know of the grisly horrors it contained.

Vampires and Monsters • Other legends of Glamis hint of vampires born into the Bowes-Lyons family which have been locked away forever from any possible contact with humans; or of a half-human monster, possibly a first-born son and heir to the title of Earl of Strathmore who was deprived of his rightful inheritance and title because of his hideous, monstrous appearance. Whether there is any truth to these legends is not known. known.

What *is* known is that Glamis Castle contains many secret rooms, chambers and hallways. In 1849, a previously unknown staircase was found and bricked up, as was a hidden fireplace that was discovered in another room.

Patrick Lyon, Lord Strathmore (1642-1695) was probably responsible for most of the early reconstruction done on Glamis Castle. Because he was not exactly the king's most loyal servant, Patrick decided to rebuild certain sections of the castle to include secret rooms and passageways which could offer protection for himself, his secret documents, papers, and valuables, and his family as well, if the need arose.

Still, the existence of hidden rooms and closets and secret staircases and passageways does not explain why the Earls of Strathmore have so jealously guarded their family secret, or why it terrifies them so. It tells us, in fact, no more than we already knew: that Glamis Castle, in Forfarshire, Scotland, is one of the strangest and most fascinating places in the entire world.

THE BROWN MOUNTAIN LIGHTS

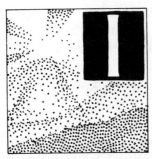

N THE NORTHERN SECTOR OF Pisgah National Forest in western North Carolina, there's a scenic overlook on Highway 105 that is known as Wiseman's View. Like any of the hundreds of other overlooks in the Blue Ridge Mountains, Wiseman's View offers sightseers a panorama of breathtaking splendor and incredible beauty. Standing along the edge of the overlook on a crisp summer day, gazing serenely out upon an endless landscape of evergreens and wildflowers below, one is reminded of the feelings expressed by naturalist John Muir upon witnessing such an inspiring view elsewhere:

"You can feel nature's peace flowing through you."

Unlike other overlooks in the area, however, Wiseman's View offers sightseeing opportunities that draw crowds of eager spectators long after darkness has overtaken the setting sun. A sign erected by the U.S. National Park Service explains the phenomenon:

BROWN MOUNTAIN LIGHTS
THE LONG, EVEN-CRESTED MTN. IN THE DISTANCE IS BROWN MTN. FROM EARLY TIMES PEOPLE HAVE OBSERVED WEIRD, WAVERING LIGHTS RISE ABOVE THIS MTN., THEN DWINDLE AND FADE AWAY.

First seen and reported by white men in 1771, the mysterious lights atop Brown Mountain have since been seen by enough people to fill Yankee Stadium ten times over. Over the years, the mountain and its dancing, shimmering lights have been studied, photographed, discussed, and written about until they now qualify as a true American legend. Yet they have been taken seriously enough to be studied on two different occasions by the United States Geological Survey, and by members of the Smithsonian Institution, the U.S. Weather Bureau, and the American Meteorological Association.

Although frequently seen, the Brown Mountain lights do not occur with clockwork regularity; they do not follow any kind of predictable pattern of appearance. Sometimes they are there, and sometimes they are not; but they are never seen anywhere except atop Brown Mountain. When they appear, they can be observed from a distance but not from up close. Aside from the obvious difficulty of climbing and searching the thickly forested mountain at night, the lights inevitably fade from view or simply blink off like giant fireflies whenever anyone approaches them. Sometimes they even rise in the air and burst into skyrocket-like flares of brilliant red, pink, or white light before disappearing.

From a distant vantage point such as the overlooks at Wiseman's View or the Grandfather Mountain area, however, the lights are clearly visible. They shine like ghostly headlights seen from afar as they move up and down and across the long, flat crest of the mountain, appearing and disappearing in such random fashion that the number of lights seen at any one time varies considerably.

The color of the lights ranges from pale blue, to white, to glowing yellow, to pink, to bright red. Sometimes they are stationary rather than moving, and sometimes they appear brighter than at other times. Even when seen at their dimmest, though, they are brighter than the brightest stars in the sky—except the sun, of course.

Brown Mountain lies in the foothills of the Blue Ridge Mountains. It is not a particularly high mountain: at 2,600 feet in elevation, its summit is 4,000 feet lower than that of Mount Mitchell, twenty-five miles to the southeast. Located in Burke County, North Carolina, not far from the town of Morganton, Brown Mountain is roughly one hundred miles west of Winston-Salem. It is situated on land that, prior to the arrival of the first white settlers, was shared by the Cherokee and Catawba Indian tribes.

Even then, hundreds of years ago, the Indians were

aware of the eerie, unpredictable lights on top of Brown Mountain. According to Cherokee legend, their tribe and the Catawbas once fought a fierce battle near Brown Mountain. Many Indian braves were slain in the bloody encounter, and when they failed to return their women went searching for them. And now, many centuries later, the spirits of those Indian women still prowl back and forth across the mountain, searching in vain for the men they lost—or so the legend says.

A variation of this legend, from the viewpoint of the white settlers, formed the basis for a popular folk song that was recorded by the Kingston Trio in the 1960s. Written by Scott Weisman, the song tells of a well-to-do Southern farmer who went hunting on Brown Mountain, became lost in the dense, virgin forest, and never returned home. A slave, fearing for his master's safety, equipped himself with a lantern and went out to search for him. The old slave never found his master—but he never gave up his search, either. At night, his lantern still can be seen as his restless spirit roams the mountain.

A local variation of this story told of the disappearance around 1850 of a married woman who lived in the Brown Mountain area. For several days and nights, residents of the community searched the mountainside, thinking that the woman might have been murdered. Although they never discovered her body, members of the search party observed mysterious lights appearing over the top of the mountain at night which were unlike any of the lights carried by searchers. The story quickly spread that the lights were the dead woman's spirit, returned from an unknown grave to haunt her murderer.

Scientists, who are always skeptical when it comes to legends, tend to dismiss the local stories of wandering spirits who haunt the mountain. However, they cannot so easily dismiss the reality of the lights themselves. Too many people have seen, and even photographed, the lights on Brown Mountain for any lingering doubt to remain as to their reality.

Instead, the experts and researchers who have investigated the lights have concentrated on explaining away their existence as a natural phenomenon. Their "explanations" have been, in some cases, the same arguments that researchers have used to explain eyewitness sightings of UFOs (unidentified flying objects).

For example, one theory holds that the lights are nothing more than the reflection of locomotive headlights, or automobile headlight beams from cars traveling along mountain roads in the area, or even reflected lights from any of several nearby towns. The chief problem with this theory is that the lights were seen by both Indians and white settlers long before electric lights or any type of engine-powered vehicles appeared. Besides, a great flood passed through the Catawba Valley in 1916, washing out most of the roads and railroad beds in the vicinity, destroying railroad trestles, and knocking down electric power lines all over the valley—yet the lights continued to shine as usual, as bright as ever.

Another theory contends that the lights are will-o'-the-wisps—shifting, elusive lights sometimes seen over marshes at night, caused by the spontaneous combustion, or sudden bursting into flame, of marsh gases. But even if there were any bogs or marshy areas on or near Brown Mountain—which there aren't—this theory does not explain why the burning occurs only at night, or why the lights always vanish whenever anyone tries to observe them at close range.

Several other possible theories have been advanced to explain the presence of the ghostly lights on Brown Mountain. One, that the lights are balls of electricity known to sailors as St. Elmo's fire, won't work because, like lightning bolts, St. Elmo's fire never lingers in the air as do the Brown Mountain lights. St. Elmo's fire always grounds itself in one fashion or another—in the case of sailing vessels, by attaching itself to a mast or spar of the ship or to any unfortunate sailor who happens to be in the vicinity. Anyway, St. Elmo's fire never occurs except during thunderstorms, while the Brown Mountain lights appear during weather conditions which are the exact opposite: mild and moderate.

Even less workable is the theory that the light is fox-fire, a kind of glowing light created by the action of fungi on decaying wood and plant remains. While the lush vegetation of the Blue Ridge Mountains creates a great deal of decaying matter, the pale glow of foxfire is hardly strong enough to be seen except at very close range— and even so, there is no reason why Brown Mountain should be the only mountain in North America to pro- duce this kind of phenomenon in amounts large enough to be seen almost continuously over a period of several hundred years.

Some observers have suggested that the ghostly lights are due to the presence of moonshiners on the mountain who use the cover of darkness to produce their illegal, unstamped (and dangerously unsanitary) bootleg whis- key. But while it is likely that moonshiners probably *have* fired their stills on Brown Mountain in the past, it is unlikely that they could do so for hundreds of years, and before countless thousands of observers, without getting caught somewhere along the way. This is especially true considering the large number of individual lights that can be seen at times on or atop the mountain: to U. S. Internal Revenue agents looking to the southeast at night from the overlook at Wiseman's View, it would appear that the moonshiners were holding a national convention, complete with noiseless fireworks displays, on the long, flat summit of Brown Mountain!

Another theory suggests that the lights are similar to the "Andes Lights" associated with the great South American mountain range. In the high Andes—at elevations of 15,000 feet or higher—sometimes electrical discharges (lightning) pass through clouds to mountaintops where they shine as circular lights visible for a long way off. But although this theory was advanced by prominent officials from the U. S. Weather Bureau and the American Meteorological Association, it, too, cannot be accurate.

First, while the Andes Lights phenomenon is known to occur only at extremely high altitudes, Brown Mountain is a low-elevation mountain; in fact, it isn't even the tallest mountain in its own general vicinity. And although the Andes Lights are associated with electrical disturbances in the skies, the Brown Mountain lights occur most often under calm, cloudless skies.

In fact, none of the scientific explanations given thus far adequately explains the ghostly procession of lights seen periodically atop Brown Mountain. Perhaps they will never be fully explained or understood in scientific terms.

Still, it doesn't really matter. The Brown Mountain lights continue to shine, fascinating and mystifying viewers as they have done since the days when Indians and settlers shared the land.

Curses, Witchings,
and Ghostings

EGYPTIAN CURSES

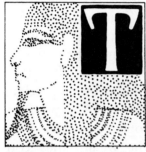

THE ANCIENT EGYPTIANS ACHIEVED A level of civilization which, by the middle of the fourteenth century B.C., was the most advanced and highly developed society that the world had ever known. They developed artificial irrigation systems to carry the waters of the Nile River to their fields. They developed a written language, hieroglyphics, and invented paper to write it on. They had advanced forms of government, commerce, and law, and were also brilliant architects, artists, metalworkers, and engineers. They even had the world's first zoos.

The ancient Egyptians believed in the existence of a great many gods. One of these was Amon-Ra (or, simply, Amon), the sun god; another was Osiris, the god of the dead.

When an Egyptian king or ruler (called a pharaoh) died, his entire body was preserved in the form of a mummy through a drying-out process similar to our embalming procedure. Then he was carefully wrapped in funeral cloths, placed in a tomb, and surrounded with fine clothing, food, jewelry, and other objects to carry with him on his long journey to the Realm of the Dead. Sometimes paintings or sculptures of servants were left in the tomb to assist and guide him on his journey; at other times, living servants were buried alive with their departed masters for the same purpose.

In either case, though, it was important that the entire body be preserved and the contents of the tomb left intact and undisturbed. If these rules were violated, the soul of the departed person could not find eternal peace with Amon-Ra in the paradise-like "field of content."

And because both the number and richness of the objects in the tomb indicated the importance of the person who had died, it was customary to fill a pharaoh's burial chamber with objects made of gold and set with precious stones of great beauty and value. At the same time, realizing the temptation for grave-robbers and thieves to break into the tombs and steal the wealth they contained, the ancient Egyptians carved warnings, or curses, above the entranceways to the burial chambers.

Typical of these threats or curses are two that were said to have been found in the tomb of the boy-king Tutankhamen, who died in 1352 B.C.: above the entrance to the tomb was an inscription that read, *Death will come to those who disturb the sleep of the Pharaohs.* And inside the tomb, at the base of a jackal-headed statue of Anubis, another Egyptian god, was an inscription that was said to read, *It is I who hold back the sand from choking the secret chamber. I protect the dead, and I will kill all who cross this threshold and enter the sacred dwelling place of the eternal Pharaoh.*

Tutankhamen was only eighteen years old when he died. He had become pharaoh six years before, at the age of twelve, and at that time he was already married to a daughter of the previous pharaoh, Ikhnaton.

Ikhnaton, who ruled Egypt for seventeen years beginning in 1375 B.C., had made one important change in

Egyptian religion: he did away with all the gods except one, which he renamed Aton, the sun god. Naturally, this change was not greeted enthusiastically by priests who were faithful to the other gods. As long as Ikhnaton lived, they had little choice but to accept and obey his word as law. But when he finally died in 1358 B.C. and Tutankhamen (sometimes referred to as "King Tut") came to power, the priests wasted little time in restoring their old gods to their former places of prominence.

Ikhnaton's religion, in which one god ruled all creation, had been so unpopular during his lifetime that one of his daughters dared to oppose him openly. In response, he had her tortured and killed. Her right hand was severed and buried apart from the rest of her body, so that her soul might never attain heavenly peace.

Some 3,250 years later, in the 1890s, a man named Count Hamon claimed to have come into possession of the mummified hand of Ikhnaton's daughter. And some years after that, on Halloween night, 1922, he claimed that he was visited in England by the spirit of the young Egyptian princess whose hand had been taken from her in death. Then, having reclaimed her hand, she disappeared instantly.

A few days later, Count Hamon read in the newspapers that a team of British archaeologists sponsored by Lord Carnarvon had discovered the location of what was thought to be the long-lost tomb of Tutankhamen. The tomb was the only such burial place of a pharaoh that was still undiscovered and unexplored as late as the 1920s; according to legend, it was filled with vast fortunes and unimagined wealth.

Count Hamon was already aware of the supposed "death curse" associated with the tomb of Tutankhamen.

And because he sensed a connection between his recent encounter with the spirit of Ikhnaton's daughter and the finding of Tutankhamen's grave, he sent an urgent warning to the archaeologists not to proceed with the excavation of the tomb. He pleaded with them not to enter it. He prophesied that, if Lord Carnarvon entered the tomb, he would "suffer sickness" from which he would ". . . not recover. Death will claim you in Egypt."

Lord Carnarvon did not entirely disregard Count Hamon's warning or the famous "curse" that was supposed to be associated with the tomb and its contents. In fact, he consulted fortunetellers at least twice: on both occasions, they predicted that his death, which was imminent, would occur under strange circumstances that would be questioned by many people. He was strongly tempted to abandon the project even at this late date, but he was talked out of quitting by Howard Carter, the leader of the expedition that Lord Carnarvon was financing. Carter wasn't willing to abandon the most exciting discovery of his career. He persuaded his wealthy partner to continue, and on Febuary 22, 1923, Lord Carnarvon stepped into the opened tomb for the first time. Except for some grave robbers who were caught forcing their way into the tomb during the time of the pharaohs, he became the first person to challenge the ancient curse in more than three thousand years. He was followed into the tomb by an eager Howard Carter.

Inside, they found treasures that were more fabulous than their wildest dreams could have conjured up and wealth that was greater by far than the legends had foretold. Gold was everywhere—gold, and more precious gemstones than could be imagined. Golden daggers inlaid with gems and ivory, and golden tables, chairs and thrones, golden necklaces and earrings and bracelets and replicas of gods. A magnificent golden sarcophagus surrounded an inner coffin of gold. Beneath that, covering the mummified remains of the boy-king, was a splendid death mask of gold, lapis lazuli, and cut glass. It was formed in the exact likeness of Tutankhamen, who was an exceedingly handsome young man.

Forty-two days after he first stepped into the tomb of "King Tut," Lord Carnarvon was dead, the victim of . . . a mosquito bite. He was 57 years old when he died. (It was widely rumored that the mummy had a mark on its cheek in the same exact spot where Lord Carnarvon was

bitten by the mosquito that carried a fatal disease.)

His son, Lord Porchester, the sixth Earl of Carnarvon, said that as his father lay dying in Egypt, back in England his father's dog began howling mournfully. It ceased its howling only when the two of them—the dog and its master—died at same time, as verified later by family members and household staff in Egypt and England. And at the precise moment of Lord Carnarvon's death in Cairo, Egypt, his son related, the lights failed and the entire city of Cairo was plunged into darkness momentarily. Whether it was a coincidence or otherwise, no one ever discovered the cause for the blackout and loss of electricity.

Thus began the famous "Curse of King Tut," which brought with it death, misfortune, or injury to many of those who defied the curse and assisted in the removal of the contents of the burial chamber.

From the time King Tut's tomb was opened, worldwide press coverage of the historic event was divided between the incredible treasures that were being unearthed almost daily and the bizarre and ominous series of tragedies that seemed to plague the expedition literally from Lord Carnarvon's first steps inside the tomb.

Two men—one was Arthur Mace, an American archaeologist on the expedition, and the other a technician who X-rayed the mummy—complained of extreme fatigue, collapsed, and died shortly thereafter. Two other men who visited the tomb during that time died from a mysterious high fever, one of them less than two days after he first entered the tomb. (Admittedly, the man was ill even before he traveled to Egypt.) Lord Carnarvon's personal secretary on the excavation was found in his bed, dead from a heart attack.

By 1930, seven years after the tomb was first re-opened, twenty-two of the original forty excavators were dead. And while many of them were in their forties or fifties, it does appear to be a rather high mortality rate.

Other fatalities have been attributed to the curse. Two Egyptian national directors of antiquities met their deaths (in 1966 and 1972) as they prepared to send the Tutankhamen treasures out of Egypt on separate world-wide tours. And of the flight crew that transported the Tutankhamen exhibition to England in 1972, the pilot later died suddenly of a heart attack at age forty, the flight engineer died at age forty-five (after his seventh heart attack), and one of the stewards later suffered two non-fatal heart attacks, although he was only thirty-five years old. Another member of the crew lost his home and belongings in a fire; another broke his foot shortly after he kicked the box which contained the famous, exquisite death mask of Tutankhamen; and a sixth member of the crew resigned her air force commission after undergoing a serious operation.

Could all of this have occurred by chance?

Yes, comes the reply from those people who refuse to believe in the existence of any "curse" of Tutankhamen's tomb. As evidence, they point to the fact that the true leader of the expedition, Howard Carter, lived seventeen years after the opening of the tomb, surviving until 1939 when he died at age sixty-six.

They also contend that there *is* no "curse," but merely incorrect translations of the hieroglyphics—made perhaps by those who wished to believe in the existence of such exciting notions as "curses." They translate the in-scription this way: *It is I who hinder the sand from choking the secret chamber. I am for the protection of the deceased.* And they point out that many of those who died either were old in the first place, or else they died of natural causes.

The Strangest Curse of All • Probably the most effective curse of all time was the inscription found on an ornament that adorned the mummified remains of a high priestess of Amon-Ra. The inscription itself was mild enough. It read: *Awaken from your sleeping dream and you will conquer all that act against you.*

In life, the high priestess had been a prophetess or seer, capable of foretelling the future. She lived during the reign of Ikhnaton.

In death, her mummified form occupied a gold-and-enamel mummy case that revealed her importance in the ancient Egyptian way of life and death. Who could have foretold the pain, tragedy, even death the priestess would bring to virtually everyone who touched the mummy case she was in, or so much as came near her after she left Egypt?

Her remains, including the mummy case or coffin, were eventually bought by a man named Douglas Murray, who lived to regret the experience. A week after he purchased the mummy and its case and had it shipped to London, a gun exploded in his hand, causing the eventual loss of that hand. Two of his companions on his trip to Egypt were less fortunate: they died on the way home.

The curse had begun to work with deadly effect.

The two Egyptian workers in Cairo who had packed the mummy in its case, crated it up for delivery to London, and carted it onto the ship, died within the year. And Mr. Murray was said to have believed that the carved eyes on the mummy case were alive and watching him. Eventually, he gave the mummy to a woman who immediately began to suffer a series of personal setbacks and health problems. She quickly returned it to Murray, who in turn gave it to the British Museum.

In the process of having ownership transferred to the museum, two more people died—and after the museum accepted the mummy, so many complaints were received about accidents and mysterious goings-on in the vicinity of the mummy's display that museum personnel finally moved the mummy and her case to the basement.

Eventually, the British Museum solved its problem by offering the mummy to a New York museum, which accepted it gratefully.

Thus it was that, in 1912, the valuable Egyptian mummy was on its way across the Atlantic, bound for a new home in New York City. Captain Ernest Smith rightly considered the irreplaceable property too valuable to store in the ship's hold, where it might be damaged; instead, the crate was brought to the bridge where the captain could look after it personally. He did, too—some say he looked after it too well, when he should have been looking after his ship.

Nearly 1,500 lives were lost—1,493, to be precise— when on Monday, April 15, 1912, the *Titanic* hit an iceberg and sank in the frigid waters of the north Atlantic Ocean.

The high priestess's mummy never was recovered from its watery grave two and one-half miles below the surface of the icy Atlantic. Perhaps it never will be. Maybe it shouldn't be recovered: after all, she is at rest now. And since the fateful night of April 15, 1912, no one else has fallen prey to the curse that has remained with her mummy for nearly 2,400 years.

THE BELL WITCH

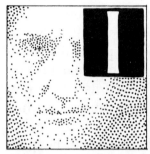I T ALL BEGAN ONE FINE AUTUMN day in 1817. The scene was a cornfield on the 1,000-acre farm of John Bell, which was located on the south bank of the Red River near Adams, Tennessee. Mr. Bell, a hard-working, well-to-do farmer, husband, and father of eight children, was walking alone in his cornfield when he spotted a dog-like animal nearby. It wasn't a dog, though, nor was it any other kind of animal Mr. Bell had ever seen. Not knowing what else to do, he raised his gun and fired at the creature, but apparently missed it. Without moving, the animal simply faded away like a puff of smoke.

A few days later, Mr. Bell saw another animal he thought to be a wild turkey. He rushed inside his house to get his gun, but when he returned the bird was already flying away, out of shooting range. By the size of its broad, flapping wings, he could tell that the enormous bird was much larger than a turkey, or buzzard, or any other bird that he knew of.

After that, strange occurrences began happening inside the Bell house, which was a large and spacious log cabin. Family members began hearing eerie, scratching sounds in the night like a dog pawing at the doors and windows, and chewing sounds as if a rat were gnawing on their bedposts. Then, one night, as twelve-year-old Betsy Bell lay sleeping peacefully in her bed, the bedcovers were ripped away and something unseen began to strike her in the face and pull her hair. Her screams awakened the rest of the family, and when they arrived they found her hysterical. Her face was covered with angry red welts.

Soon, other family members received similar attacks. One night in particular, six-year-old Williams Bell and his older brother Joel were awakened at the same time by their covers being jerked away from them. They began to scream as they felt their noses being pinched, their hair pulled, and their faces slapped. (Later, as an adult, Williams wrote that they not only felt the sharp, painfully hard slaps, but they could *hear* the open-handed blows that they both received.) Meanwhile, Betsy was shrieking in agonized terror in her room from a similar attack on her.

The attacks and disturbances—sounds of lips smacking or of gulping or strangling, or of knocking, clawing or gnawing—continued until finally, in desperation, John Bell invited a neighbor over to witness the activities. The neighbor, a lay preacher named James Johnson, listened to the ghostly noises and then commanded them to cease in the name of the Lord.

And they *did* stop—for about a week. Then the attacks began again, usually on young Betsy. But at least the Bells knew now that the ghost, or whatever it was, could hear them and understood what was said.

Soon, the attacks on Betsy became more frequent and more violent—on more than one occasion, the ghost either jabbed her with straight pins, or else it hid them in her pillow with the sharp ends pointing out. Mr. Bell decided to send Betsy to stay with neighbors until the disturbance passed. But wherever she went, the attacks and disturbances followed her, tormenting her without letup, although they continued at home as well. All that sending Betsy away from home accomplished was to let everyone in the area know about the terrible, ghostly haunting, whereas before it had been a family secret.

At about the time that Betsy returned home, the ghost began to whistle in reply to questions that were put to it. Gradually, the whistling became whispering, and the whispering eventually became spoken words, as if the ghost were finding its voice for the first time. According to at least one source, the first words it spoke were, "Lordy, I sure am glad I can talk now; I've been waiting for this for a long time!"

Once it began talking, though, it quickly made up for lost time. While the attacks, disturbances, and other ghostly activities had been confined to the nighttime, the unseen woman's voice might be heard at any time of day or night.

John Bell and his family wasted no time in trying to communicate with the ghost. She appeared to be happy to oblige them by answering their questions, although they soon learned that she didn't always tell the truth.

When they asked her who she was and what she wanted, she replied, "I am nothing more nor less than old Kate Batts' witch, and I'm determined to haunt and torment Old Jack Bell as long as he lives." (Kate Batts was a local woman who hated John Bell because she felt that he had cheated her in a business deal—but Kate Batts was still alive at the time; in fact, she outlived John Bell by many years.) Thus the ghost, who said that she would not rest until Old Jack was dead, became popularly known as "Old Kate, the Bell Witch."

On other occasions, Old Kate gave other explanations for her presence in the Bell household. One night she told her listeners, "I am a spirit from everywhere . . . I'm in the air, in houses, any place at anytime. I've been created millions of years."

At another time she said, "I am a spirit; I once was very happy but have been disturbed." She went on to say that she had been buried nearby, but that somehow one of her teeth was lost somewhere under the Bell house. She was looking for her tooth.

The Bells mounted a massive search for the missing tooth, but never found it. The witch finally confessed gleefully that she had made up the story to tease Old Jack.

By now, word had spread far and wide concerning the remarkable goings-on at the Bell farm. Visitors were numerous and frequent, as were tests to prove that none of what was seen or heard was fake. In one such test, a doctor placed his hand over Betsy's mouth while the witch was speaking, to prove that Betsy wasn't throwing her voice like a ventriloquist. She wasn't.

When the witch accepted the visitors kindly, as she often did, she would talk with them for hours, or entertain them by singing hymns or reciting scriptures. (She seemed to know the Bible as well as a preacher.) If she didn't like them, though, she was likely to snatch off their glasses, pull their noses, or even lash them with an invisible strap.

Old Kate may have hated Betsy's father intensely and punished Betsy and her brothers often, but she never had anything but the highest praise for Lucy Bell, who was Betsy's mother. "Old Luce," the witch was fond of saying, "is the most perfect woman living." The witch often sang to Mrs. Bell, attended her Bible study meet-

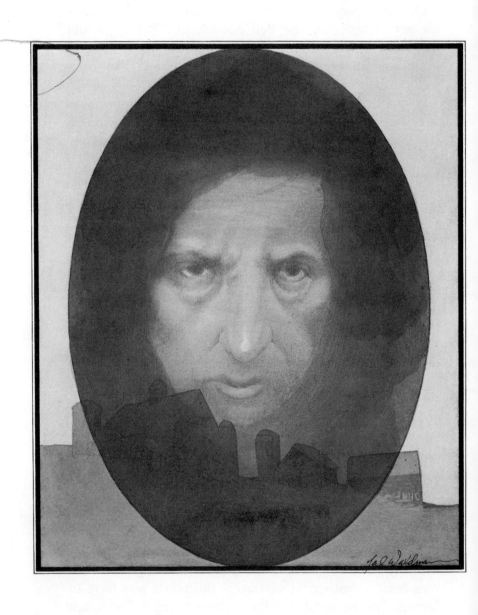

ings, and even brought refreshments in the form of fruit which she dropped into the laps of her surprised guests. And when Lucy was ill, the witch, who had no power of healing, brought her hazelnuts and even shelled them for her.

The witch attended church services regularly, and she never failed to make her presence known. At Sunday services, prayer meetings, revivals—she could always be heard, bellowing "Amens" and "Hallelujahs" at appropriate moments. She referred to the minister, who was none other than the Bells' neighbor, James Johnson, as "Old Sugar Mouth." Once, during a prayer, she blurted out, "Lordy, how sweet Old Sugar Mouth prays! How I *do* love to hear him!"

Another thing that appealed to Old Kate was moonshine whiskey. Often she would be heard arriving at the Bell house or another in the vicinity, staggering and stumbling over things, stinking up the house with her whiskey breath, and shouting drunkenly and cursing like a sailor. Apparently, she was a hard-drinking ghost who couldn't handle the stuff very well. Others besides her unwilling hosts dreaded her unwelcome visits: moonshiners in the area complained that Old Kate often raided their stills and stole moonshine from them.

Old Kate became famous as a local gossip. She knew *everything* that happened to everyone in the community, and she loved nothing better than to spread the word concerning who was sinning, and what sins they were committing, to anyone who was eager to hear it. That fact added greatly to the ever-growing number of daily visitors to the Bell cabin.

Far and wide—to the eastern and western borders of Tennessee, up into Kentucky and as far south as

Alabama—people were hearing strange tales of a ghostly witch (or witch-like ghost) who could tell listeners exactly what was happening somewhere else at the same time. Many curious people undertook long trips to see the Bell witch, and she seldom disappointed them.

One of the most famous visitors to meet Old Kate was General Andrew Jackson, the hero of the Battle of New Orleans in 1814 who later became the seventh president of the U.S. Jackson traveled from "The Hermitage," his plantation home near Nashville, together with some friends and a "witch layer" whose talent was "laying witches to rest."

As Jackson's wagon approached the Bell property, he and his friends were discussing ghosts when suddenly the wagon they were in jerked to a halt. The driver urged the horses on and lashed them, but they couldn't move. It was as if the wagon and horses were mired in thick, deep mud—but there was no mud.

Suddenly, a woman's voice rang out (although none of the women present had spoken): "All right, General, the wagon can move on now. I'll see you tonight."

"By thunder," the general shouted, "it's the witch!" Then, as if bidden to do so, the wagon began to move again, and proceeded the rest of the way to the Bells' farm without difficulty.

That night after supper, Old Kate wasted no time in getting to the point. She arrived on the scene as the witch layer was telling everyone how he was going to shoot the witch with a silver bullet.

"All right, General, here I am, ready for business," Old Kate said. Then, to the witch layer, she added, "Now, Mr. Smarty, go ahead and shoot."

The man aimed his pistol at the spot where the sound

was coming from and pulled the trigger. The gun jammed and wouldn't fire.

"Try again," the ghost suggested. He did, but with no better luck than before. The gun simply wouldn't fire.

"It's *my* turn now," Kate warned. "Look out, you old hypocrite; I'm going to teach you a lesson!"

Seconds later, a loud, sharp *smack!* was heard, and the witch layer staggered backward and fell flat. Just as quickly he leaped to his feet and began rushing helter-skelter around the room.

"My nose, my nose!" he shouted in a nasal twang, "Oh, Lord, it's got me by the nose!" Then the front door burst open by itself, and the man raced outside. The last anyone saw of him, he was hightailing it up the country road, shouting and whooping as he went that the Devil himself was after him.

General Jackson left the next day. Although "Old Hickory," as he was known, had enjoyed his visit, not everyone in his party was equally taken with Old Kate. Indeed, Jackson's parting words to the Bells were, "I'd rather fight the British again than have any more dealings with that torment."

Eventually, the haunting seemed to localize around two persons: John ("Old Jack") Bell, whom the witch hated, and Betsy Bell, who was quickly maturing into a rather beautiful young woman.

Concerning John Bell, Old Kate seldom missed an opportunity to bother, irritate, or injure him. He often complained of being stuck with needles and pins or, without warning, of being slapped, struck, whipped, or beaten by unseen hands and invisible straps, belts, or sticks. The witch kept him awake at night by shouting insults and cursing at him; she made his life a torment.

Not long after General Jackson's visit, John Bell began suffering from "spells," or fits and convulsions, in which his face would jerk, twist, and twitch uncontrollably.

His tongue grew swollen until he could scarcely eat, speak, or breathe. These "spells" were accompanied by physical attacks in which he would be knocked down and struck in the face repeatedly by the unseen witch. The power of her attacks and the spells he was suffering finally forced him to bed around early December, 1820. His condition continued to worsen until, on the morning of December 20, he quietly passed away.

Old Kate quickly and proudly took the blame for John Bell's death. "It's useless to try to revive Old Jack," she said. "He'll never get up."

She told her listeners that she had poisoned him the night before. And when a mysterious medicine bottle was found in the cupboard where the medicine was kept, she said that it contained the poison that she had used on him. For once, Old Kate appeared to be telling the truth.

Not content with having murdered her sworn enemy, Kate showed up for John Bell's funeral, too. As his casket was lowered into the ground she began singing loudly, "Row me up some brandy, oh . . ."

A short time after her father's death, Betsy Bell became engaged to a young man named Josiah ("Josh") Gardener. They loved each other very much, and both families were pleased to hear of their wedding plans. But not Old Kate. She was dead set against the wedding and set out to destroy it.

"Please, please, Betsy Bell, don't marry Josh Gardener," she urged in a loud, pleading tone. She constantly embarrassed the two of them when they were together, cursing, playing evil tricks on others, and reminding Betsy that *this* was what the rest of her life would be like if she married Josh.

Finally, in desperation after four years of the witch's torment and bedevilment, Betsy could stand no more abuse. She broke off her engagement to Josh. He took the sad news bravely because he understood what she had been through, and they parted ways forever.

This act seemed to satisfy Old Kate. When Betsy later married a much older man named Richard Powell, the witch made no objection. Having satisfied herself with her actions regarding John and Betsy Bell, the witch seemed to lose interest in the Bell family.

One evening in the spring of 1821, she abruptly announced to the family, "Goodby, I am going, and will be gone for seven years." And she left, just like that.

She kept her promise, and reappeared briefly in 1828. This time, though, she was not as violently evil as before: although she still enjoyed snatching the bedcovers off sleeping family members every now and then, she did not attack them or try to hurt them. And she told John, Jr., that this time she would not be back for 107 years.

Many years later, in 1935, the Bell family of that time was braced for the return visit which Old Kate had promised way back in 1828. But 1935 passed without any appearances by the ghost, after which many a sigh of relief was heard among the descendants of John Bell.

During the four years of Old Kate's visitation in the Bell home and surrounding community, the Bells never failed to open their doors to a single person who wanted to see for himself what was going on. More than anything else, the family wanted their dreaded, mean-tempered guest to leave. They welcomed anyone who might know how to get rid of Old Kate.

Hundreds of investigators came and went during the years 1817-1821. They conducted every test they could think of to prove that Old Kate wasn't real, or that the family was "faking" the tricks that Old Kate performed. None of them succeeded. What's more, none of them ever came up with a single clue as to why Old Kate appeared; or why she hated John Bell so bitterly; or why she did not want Betsy to marry Josh Gardener; or why, after more than four years, she suddenly left as quickly as she came.

There is, of course, the psychical theory that the cause of the disturbance was Betsy Bell, who was acting as the "focus person" for the poltergeist activity of "Old Kate." But Betsy was a gentle, soft-spoken person, and her father John was, by all accounts, a fine man who loved his wife and children very much. Could Betsy have directed her psychic energy against her father and herself so violently that her father died as a result, while she herself suffered countless ghostly beatings and the loss of her fiance?

No one in Betsy's family thought that *that* was the case. Of course, no one will ever know for sure.

Or will they?

Old Kate promised in 1828 that she would return again in 107 years. She didn't return as promised . . . but maybe she *will* come back someday; after all, it wouldn't be the first time that she ever stretched the truth.

THE DEVIL'S FOOTPRINTS

 MONG THE MOST DIFFICULT OCCULT experiences to understand or explain are those which occur once, and then are seen or heard no more. One memorable case of this sort occurred during the night of February 8, 1855, in five towns of south Devonshire, England.

After a heavy snowfall that night, residents and shopkeepers emerged from their homes next morning to find mysterious tracks in the newly fallen snow. The small, horseshoe-shaped tracks measured two inches wide and four inches long, and were spaced precisely eight inches apart.

Even more curiously, the tracks were arranged in single file, as if whatever made them had either hopped on one foot, or walked or galloped by placing one foot directly in front of the other.

The tracks were seen throughout each of the towns, in one continuous path measuring sixty miles long. When they reached a wall, they either continued on top of the wall or proceeded on the other side, as if the creature had hopped or flown from the one spot to the other. And that was strange, too: if you've ever hopped or jumped in deep snow, you're aware that the act of jumping or landing in snow affects *both* footprints, the one where you take off from and the one where you land. They're deeper than your normal, walking footprints in snow (due to the force your body generates as you take off and land), and your footprints invariably are smudged around the front or back edges, making those footprints appear larger than the others. But these tiny footprints were the same depth and size everywhere, even when it appeared that their maker must have leaped over a high wall—and nowhere were they spaced any more or less than eight inches apart!

Investigators estimated that, for one creature to make the single set of continuous tracks—as appeared to have been the case—it would have had to complete the sixty miles involved in something like half a day. And with each step covering only eight inches, the creature must have been moving at the unbelievable rate of nearly ten steps per second, including its efforts to avoid obstacles in its path such as walls and fences.

Even the fastest animals on earth cannot duplicate that kind of movement. The peregrine falcon, which is the world's fastest-flying bird, has been timed at speeds of more than 160 miles per hour—but only in the air, not running in snow. The cheetah, the fastest land animal on earth, has been clocked at 60 miles per hour—but at full stride and in short bursts, not in tiny, eight-inch steps covering sixty miles.

Experts ruled out every conceivable animal in the area, including cats, dogs, birds, rats, horses, cows, frogs, rabbits, foxes, otters, badgers, chickens, skunks, ducks, geese, sheep, pigs, and even kangaroos (from a local zoo), deciding for various reasons that none of these could be the culprit.

None of those animals—or, for that matter, any other known animal on earth—makes normal, walking footprints in a single, straight path (rather than making *two* straight paths) without displaying right and left feet. (Try it yourself by walking barefoot in soft sand and studying the footprints you leave behind you.) None of those animals (or any other) can hop on one foot for sixty miles at a time. And no animal gallops and leaps onto walls and over fences for sixty miles without at least occasionally taking steps that are longer or shorter than others.

It's clear, too, that the mysterious event could not have been a trick or practical joke played by one or more unidentified persons, since no human-sized footprints or tracks were found in the freshly fallen snow. Anyway, what kind of practical joker would take the time and effort to measure and set down, in deep snow and at night, more than 420,000 separate, false footprints? And how could such a feat be accomplished without anyone noticing the culprit at work?

If you're confused about all this, think how the residents of south Devonshire must have felt. Many of them were terrified that they had been visited by strange, unearthly beings or tiny monsters or creatures from another world. Some locked themselves indoors, fearing that they were victims of the Devil's handiwork.

The incident was never repeated.

Eventually, the townspeople were able to put their fears behind them and return to their normal lives. But because no one has ever been able to come up with any kind of sensible solution to the mystery, the story of the Devil's Footprints remains one of the most incredible unexplained events in recorded history.

THE BLACK CAT

WHEN MRS. MARGARET O'BRIEN AND her husband Nicholas bought the building in Killakee, Ireland, known as the Dower House in 1968, they knew they were purchasing a house with a strange and evil history behind it.

The 200-year-old building, which was originally called the Massey dower house, was part of the old Massey estate; in the late 1800s, it had been the meeting place of a weird society known as the Order of the Golden Dawn. This group had met periodically to practice ceremonial magic, and possibly devil-worship as well.

However, the sinister history of the Dower House goes back a great deal further than that.

In 1735, a group of local young men founded a club for devil-worship which met in a hunting lodge on the summit of Mount Pelier behind the Dower House. There they gambled, held wild, drunken orgies, and performed Black Masses in honor of their Master of Darkness. On one occasion, some of them were rumored to have murdered a crippled, deformed servant.

The leader in this act of unspeakable cruelty was a wealthy young man named Thomas "Buck" Whaley. While he and several of his bloodthirsty young friends were at the Dower House, they were said to have set fire to the servant because they thought it would be fun to watch him burn.

Still, it was only a local rumor, that was all. Just a rumor. Until . . .

Shortly after the O'Briens moved into the Dower House in 1968, they began making rather extensive alterations and repairs in order to turn part of the fifteen-room house into an art center, which it is today. While three of the O'Briens' friends were staying at the house during that time, they saw the figure of a small, deformed boy standing in a doorway. As they watched him, he dissolved into the shape of a huge black cat, and then disappeared altogether.

Not long after that, workmen discovered a small brass statue of the Devil tucked away beneath a flagstone. And while they were digging on the grounds, they unearthed the skeleton of a small, deformed boy.

The Black Cat of Killakee was heard of as early as the mid-1700s, when it is said that a huge black cat was worshipped as the Devil's stand-in when he was not present at the Black Masses that were held in his honor. And when the Dower House was built during that century, the stone carving of a cat was prominently displayed among other carvings in the walls of the house.

For the past four or five decades, numerous sightings of a large, ghostly black cat have been reported in and around the town of Killakee, which lies in County Dublin in southern Ireland. Most of these sightings have occurred in the Dower House or its gardens.

Mrs. O'Brien had heard the stories, of course—but she never believed them until one day when she saw the cat herself. It was sitting in a hallway when she first saw it, as black as coal and as large as a medium-sized dog. On other occasions, she managed to catch glimpses of the cat as it disappeared into the thick, overgrown shrubbery in the garden.

Three workmen who were renovating the house had an even stranger and more frightening tale to tell.

Tom McAssey was an artist friend of Mrs. O'Brien's. Along with two other local men, he was helping to redecorate the ballroom and hallway one dark and lonely night in March, 1968. They had been at work in the hall when, according to McAssey's account, the room suddenly grew cold. McAssey had just finished locking the front door, but one of the men remarked that the front door was open.

Sure enough, the door that McAssey had just bolted shut from the inside was standing wide open. A cold breeze whispered through the dark opening—but that was not all: outside, just beyond the doorway wreathed in blackness, stood a dark, shadowy figure.

"I thought somebody was playing a joke," McAssey said, "and I said 'Come in. I see you.'"

Then all three men heard a deep, guttural growl of the sort made by a large cat such as a lion or tiger, and McAssey heard an eerie voice say, *"You don't see me. You don't even know who I am. Leave the door open."* (The other two men thought the voice was speaking in a foreign language.)

Thoroughly frightened by now, the three men panicked and rushed out of the room.

"We slammed the heavy door behind us," McAffey said, "and halfway across the room I turned and looked back. The door was open again, and a monstrous black

cat crouched in the hall, watching me with red-flecked, amber eyes."

Another painter who displays his art at Killakee Art Centre is Val McGann. Mr. McGann lives nearby, and he too has seen the ghostly black cat. He has described the creature as being as large as an Airedale (a breed of dog that stands about 23 inches tall at the shoulder), with "terrible eyes."

These and other ghostly goings-on at the Dower House—crashing sounds in the night, the mournful howling of dogs, property destroyed, and apparitions of nuns that appeared and disappeared before the witnesses' very eyes—eventually led the O'Briens to seek an exorcism of the house by a local priest. The exorcism, or casting out of evil spirits or demons by ritual prayer, was performed in the summer of 1968. For about a year after that, things were calm and uneventful at the Dower House and the Art Centre.

Then, in late 1969 or early 1970, a group of actor friends of the O'Briens held a seance in the house, after which the ghostly disturbances returned in the form of noises at night. These were so loud and unsettling that the O'Briens and their guests were driven to consult a medium in hopes of finding out what was causing the disturbances.

The medium told Mrs. O'Brien a very strange thing: she said that it would be best to get rid of a metal figure of a cat which had been found on the premises and placed over the entrance to the art gallery.

According to the medium, the brass cat had once adorned the gravestone of a small, deformed boy who died at the Dower House under horrible circumstances more than 150 years ago. But while the medium's story was identical to the legend in every respect, it did nothing to get rid of the strange and terrifying noises that were plaguing the Art Centre.

In desperation, Mrs. O'Brien turned to a priest who was visiting the area. He told her that the medium's presence had upset the "spirits" within the house, and that the disturbances would lessen when the medium left. Then either he or another priest performed a second exorcism, after which the disturbances gradually ceased altogether.

Some people believe that the quiet at the Dower House is only temporary, and that things never will be entirely normal in the house or in the area around Killakee. There is simply too much history of evil there, they say, from the tales of devil-worship in the 1700s to the horrifying modern appearances of the huge, ghostly black cat.

It's still there, some local people insist: an enormous dark shape, the Devil's cat, lurking in the blackest shadows just beyond the fringes of light. Its amber glowing eyes burn with eternal hatred of mankind as it watches—and waits—until the time is ripe to show itself again.

Mysteries at Sea

THE DISAPPEARANCE OF FLIGHT 19

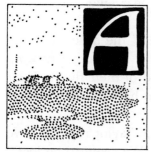T 2:00 P.M. ON DECEMBER 5, 1945, FIVE U.S. Navy planes—torpedo bombers, fully equipped with the latest and best in radio and navigational equipment—took off from the Naval Air Station at Fort Lauderdale, Florida.

The group of TBM Avengers designated as Flight 19 was on a routine training mission that would take them on a traingular route 160 miles to the east over the Atlantic Ocean, 40 miles to the north, and then southwest and back to the base at Fort Lauderdale.

There was nothing to indicate that Flight 19 would be different from any of the other training missions undertaken at the Naval Air Station every day. Granted, the area of the Atlantic over which they were flying—known popularly as the "Bermuda Triangle"—had for more than two centuries been the site of countless unexplained disappearances. But this was to be a short flight of two hours or less, and the sky was clear overhead, the ocean calm below. Besides, the fourteen crew members aboard the five planes were familiar with the area. All of them had made the same trip many times before.

At 3:45 P.M., when the planes of Flight 19 should have

been calling the tower for landing instructions, there was no word from the bomber group. Tower personnel began trying to reach Flight 19. After several failed attempts, they finally reached the young flight leader, Lieutenant Charles Taylor. His words were garbled by static and interference, and therefore were difficult to understand: "Calling Tower, this is an emergency. We seem to be off course. We cannot see land. Repeat, we cannot see land."

"What is your position, Flight 19?" the base air traffic controller asked. The planes should have been nearing the Naval Air Station at the tail end of their flight. Their flying speed for the mission was to have been 200 miles per hour.

"We are not sure of our position," Taylor replied. "We can't be sure of just where we are. We seem to be lost."

"Fly due west," the controller suggested. "In a few minutes you'll sight the mainland."

There was a pause. Then: "We do not know which way is west. Everything is wrong . . . strange. Even the ocean doesn't look as it should."

The static grew worse, and the controller at the Naval Air Station could hardly make out what was said as the men in the planes began talking to each other. For some unknown reason, the flight commander, Lieutenant Taylor, turned command over to another pilot. A few minutes later, at 4:25 P.M., a brief message reached the tower from Flight 19: "Still not certain where we are, but believe we are about 225 miles southeast of base. Looks like we are—"

And that was it. The message was never completed.

Convinced by now that a potentially serious problem was developing, base personnel hastily sent out a huge

Martin Mariner flying boat with a crew of thirteen experienced airmen aboard to search for the missing flight group. Leader of this search-and-rescue mission was Lieutenant Robert Cox, the Naval Air Station's senior flight instructor.

Practically as soon as the rescue plane was in the air, Lieutenant Cox radioed the missing planes: "I'll fly south to meet you and guide you back. What's your altitude?"

The reply he received was mostly garbled and indistinct, but both he and the tower controller heard clearly the last four ominous words: "Don't come after me."

For the next seven minutes, Lieutenant Cox and his

crew maintained radio contact with the Naval Air Station as they searched the clear skies—and the ocean as well—without finding any sign of the missing planes. Then radio contact was lost and the big Martin Mariner flying boat simply vanished. It was never seen again.

The disappearance of the rescue plane brought the total to six planes lost, with twenty-seven men aboard, and triggered a massive aircraft search. In all, between 250-300 planes, twenty-one ships, numerous smaller vessels such as fishing boats and Coast Guard cutters, and at least a dozen land search parties joined the search, but to no avail. No signs of the lost airplanes were ever found: no survivors or bodies, no debris or wreckage on land or sea, no oil slicks in the ocean where the planes might have gone down—nothing.

Never in aviation history has a case posed so many unanswered questions.

First, and most importantly, there is the obvious question: *What happened to Flight 19?*

Flight Leader Lieutenant Taylor had said, "We seem to be lost." But how could that be? All navigators aboard Flight 19 were experienced airmen. Could all of them have gotten lost at one time? Surely not. Even if the navigational equipment on all five planes had failed simultaneously —which was extremeiy unlikely—the skies were clear and they should have been able to find land by heading west as the tower controller suggested. But no; "We don't know which way is west," Lieutenant Taylor had replied. An inexperienced Boy Scout should have been able to find his way west on a clear, sunny day—and these were experienced airmen, not frightened teenagers.

There was also the fact that no SOS signal was ever received from Flight 19.

Is it possible that all five of the Avengers ran out of fuel at the same time? Or that they went down so suddenly that none of the aircraft had time to send out an emergency call for help?

If *you* were a pilot facing the prospect of crashing into the ocean, wouldn't you try to send out some kind of SOS signal requesting emergency help? Instead, the leader of Flight 19 had done exactly the opposite: he had radioed the rescue plane, "Don't come after us."

Another radio communication from the flight commander was equally puzzling and unexpected: "Everything is wrong . . . Even the ocean looks strange." *Strange* is not the kind of word one normally uses to describe the ocean. Seas may be calm, or choppy, or stormy—but they aren't strange.

The Avenger aircrafts of Flight 19 should have been able to stay afloat for several hours even after crash landing in the ocean, but apparently they didn't. Too, each of the planes was equipped with survival equipment such as self-inflating life rafts, and the men were wearing life jackets. It is virtually impossible that none of the hundreds of search vessels combing the Atlantic for weeks after the disappearance should have spotted even a single survivor, or debris of the sort that a plane crash at sea produces, or at least an oil slick—but they didn't. Their search ranged from as far north as Canada to Bermuda and Puerto Rico to the east, to the Bahamas to the south, yet they never turned up a single clue as to the fate of the missing planes and airmen.

Other questions concern the Martin Mariner rescue plane. It was a "flying boat" complete with pontoons for landing in water; why, then, if it had suffered engine trouble, hadn't the pilot simply set down in the ocean and awaited help? And why were there no emergency radio messages from the disabled Mariner before or after it went down? Had it, too, suffered a breakdown of its radio equipment?

The obvious answer would appear to lie in sabotage of the planes and equipment. But World War II had ended with the unconditional surrender of Japan months earlier. At the time of the disappearance of Flight 19, the United States had no enemies who were capable of sabotage of this sort—and even if such an enemy had existed, why would it confine its efforts to a single strike against six planes?

Besides, the Navy Board of Inquiry that investigated the disappearance found absolutely no evidence of sabotage in the case of Flight 19. In fact, the Board of Inquiry found no evidence that anything happened at all, except the unexplained disappearance of six planes and twenty-seven naval airmen. The board concluded, "We are not able to even make a good guess as to what happened."

In the years that have passed since the strange disappearance of Flight 19 on December 5, 1945, no further evidence has been found to explain what really happened on that fateful day. Other explanations have been suggested—that the planes were sunk by extraterrestrial aliens living in the ocean, or the crews captured by UFOs, that sort of thing—but such explanations have been considered too fantastic to merit serious attention except in the movies. In the science-fiction movie "Close Encounters of the Third Kind," for example, the disappearance of the planes and crew of Flight 19 was explained as the work of UFOs that turned out to be alien spacecraft. At the movie's conclusion, the entire crew of Flight 19 (including the men from the Martin Mariner) emerged from the aliens' Mother Ship, unharmed and not a day older than when they disappeared in 1945.

Perhaps there is another possible explanation.

The word *parapsychology* refers to the scientific study of occurrences which do not fall within the range of "normal" events governed by physical principles. It is, in other words, the science of the unexplained.

If, for example, an apple is seen to fall up rather than down, then one of two conclusions must be true: either the observer was mistaken, or else the apple was affected by forces of which we are unaware.

The general category in which we place occurrences which are beyond rational explanation by ordinary physical principles—such as the case of apples that fall up instead of down—is known as the *occult*, or the *supernatural*.

Certainly the disappearance of Flight 19 falls into this category. The naval inquiry board admitted as much in saying that it could not even hazard a guess as to what happened to the missing planes or crew.

As Sir Arthur Conan Doyle's famous detective Sherlock Holmes was fond of saying, "When you have eliminated the impossible, whatever remains, however improbable, must be the truth."

Many parapsychologists, or psychical researchers, believe that life does not end with death. They believe that spirits of the dead pass on to an "after-life" in another dimensional plane.

What if, by some mysterious set of circumstances that is beyond our understanding, the planes and crew of Flight 19 accidentally managed to pass out of our three-dimensional world and into another, presently unknown *fourth* dimension of time and space? If so, the missing crewmen could still be alive right now, trapped in a parallel universe of which we are not aware.

Considered in these terms, many of the unexplained, "other-worldly" aspects of the disappearance are easily understood. For example, the flight leader's statement that, "Everything is wrong . . . strange. Even the ocean doesn't look as it should," might have occurred as Flight 19 began its entry into the eerie other-world. Likewise, his final message to his rescuers, "Don't come after me," begins to sound more and more like a warning.

Of *course* he and his navigators would have been lost and unable to determine directions accurately: navigational equipment is not designed to steer passengers through doorways in time and space leading to other dimensional planes. And radio communication would be equally useless in trying to send messages from another, parallel dimension.

Perhaps the Martin Mariner flying boat actually did land in the ocean—but in an ocean far removed from our ability to comprehend it from this side of the grave.

Does this explanation sound fantastic? Maybe. But it certainly is no more fantastic than any of the details of the disappearance of Flight 19—a disappearance that was so bizarre, so mysterious, and so unaccountable, that it simply could not have occurred.

It happened, though.

It is a true ghost story—without ghosts.

THE TRUE STORY OF THE FLYING DUTCHMAN

OU'VE PROBABLY HEARD OF THE legendary ghost ship, the Flying Dutchman; if you have, you probably also know that, according to the legends, she is doomed to sail the seas forever, carrying with her misfortune and disaster. But do you know how the legend arose? Or why, after more than four hundred years, the legends are still believed by many experienced sailors and men of the sea?

Sometime around the year 1580, a Dutch merchant ship set sail from Amsterdam, Holland, bound for what is now known as Jakarta, Indonesia. The sailing vessel, under the command of Captain Hendrik Van der Decken, was following a route around the Cape of Good Hope at the southern tip of Africa when a fierce gale arose, whipping the sea into a frenzy and battering the ship relentlessly.

Captain Van der Decken never arrived at the port of Jakarta, and his ship was not seen again until several years later. Then crewmen aboard Dutch ships sailing west around the Cape, in calm waters under a clear sky, saw a strange, ghostly vessel in the distance. It was identified as the missing Dutch merchant ship, struggling to make headway against a terrible storm that was raging directly over it and nowhere else.

Thus began the legend of the *Flying Dutchman*, a ghost ship said to bring ill fortune or tragedy to any ship whose crew is unfortunate enough to see her.

A legend is a story that is passed along from one generation to another until it becomes part of the folklore of a people. Sometimes legends are true stories based on actual people and events, such as the American legend of Johnny Appleseed. (John Chapman, or "Johnny Appleseed," as he was called, was a frontiersman who planted apple trees throughout the American midwest between 1800-1845.) In other cases, legends are made-up stories about people who may or may not have actually lived, such as the tales of King Arthur and his knights of the Round Table. In yet other instances, legends are made-up stories of people who never lived at all, such as the tales of Paul Bunyan and his blue ox Babe.

In the case of the *Flying Dutchman*, the legend originally was based on a true incident—the disappearance of a ship and later sighting of a ghost ship in the vicinity of the Cape of Good Hope. However, as the story of the spectral ship spread throughout Europe, the details of the actual sighting grew blurred and began to take a back seat to the famous legend that arose around the incident.

Although numerous popular books and stories have been written about the ghost ship, the most famous adaptation of the legend was the opera *The Flying Dutchman* (1843) by the German composer Richard Wagner. This, in turn, was based on an earlier book, *Scenes of a Maritime Life*, which was written by Auguste Jal and published in 1832.

In Jal's story, the doomed ship was sailing around the Cape of Good Hope when a terrible storm arose. The passengers and crew begged the captain—who was a hard, cruel man—to find shelter in a port as the storm worsened. He merely laughed at them and said that no one, not even God Himself, would dare try to sink his ship.

Fearing death and considering the captain a madman, the passengers organized a mutiny and tried to take over the ship, but the captain resisted and tossed the rebellious leader overboard into the stormy seas. Suddenly, an angelic or heavenly being appeared on the deck. As the passengers and crew cowered in fear before it, the captain calmly drew his pistol, aimed carefully, and fired. The bullet struck the spirit, bounced off it, and pierced the captain's hand.

For his actions, the captain was cursed to sail the seas forever without haven or rest in any port, and without company save that of stormy seas and the Devil himself. "And since you take delight in others' misfortunes," the spirit went on, "your ship shall bring misfortune to all who see it."

That was the legend. And because the story was so popular, superstitious seamen all over the world began to blame every unexplained tragedy or misfortune that occurred at sea on sightings of the *Flying Dutchman*. If a ship ran aground or wrecked on a rocky shoreline or submerged coral reef; or if food or water was found to be spoiled or foul; or if sailors became unaccountably ill or lost at sea; you could bet that, sooner or later, the story would get around that the *Flying Dutchman* and its evil captain had claimed yet another victim.

But that's not the end of the story.

So far, all we have is a legend that ranks among the most widely known of all legends of the sea. But while many sailors' tales of sightings of the *Flying Dutchman* over the years since 1580 can be attributed to overactive imaginations, or to superstitious sailors who have had too much to drink, not all of the sightings can be dismissed so easily.

Some of the sightings, while eerie, have the unmistakable ring of truth to them.

In March, 1857, the crew and passengers aboard the sailing ship *Joseph Somers* had a chilling encounter with Captain Van der Decken and his ghostly ship.

They were sailing in the South Atlantic Ocean, in the vicinity of a group of small islands known as Tristan da Cunha, when suddenly the *Flying Dutchman* appeared. Wrapped in an eerie blue haze, the ship bore down on them with a speed that quickly overtook the *Joseph Somers*.

Crewmen and passengers later gave nervous sworn statements that, as the ghostly sailing ship drew within ramming range, they saw Captain Van der Decken himself on deck at the helm, snarling, sneering, and laughing hideously. Only at the last possible moment did he twist the wheel and swing his ship aside, missing the bow of the *Joseph Somers* by a matter of inches.

Almost immediately, a fire of unknown origin broke out aboard the passenger ship. Efforts to contain the fire failed, and it quickly consumed a major portion of the ship, including the lifeboats. Only the fortunate appearance of another, *real* ship saved the passengers and crew from certain death at sea.

On July 11, 1881, the commander of a British warship off the coast of Australia reported in his daily log entry that, during the early morning hours before sunrise, "the

Flying Dutchman crossed our bows." The spectral ship appeared to be wreathed in a mysterious red light. A total of thirteen men, including two officers, saw the apparition before it vanished suddenly in the clear, moonlit night. The commander also noted that two other ships in the accompanying squadron had requested information concerning a strange red glow in the ocean.

The log entry concluded with the sad news that the sailor who, as lookout, had first seen the ghost ship, "fell from our fore-topmast crosstrees and was killed instantly." He was buried at sea.

In May, 1866, the sailing vessel *General Grant* left Melbourne, Australia, bound for England and carrying (among other things) a rich cargo in gold. After several days at sea in which members of the crew reported seeing a ghostly sailing ship following them in the distance at night, the *General Grant* mysteriously wrecked and sank.

Four years later, with the treasure still unrecovered, the wreck was located and an attempt was made to salvage the fortune in gold aboard the *General Grant.*

After locating the sunken ship, several divers went down to search for the gold. None of them ever returned. What happened to them is a mystery—but no more so than what was happening above the surface at the same time!

While the salvage craft lay peacefully at anchor, a phantom ship suddenly appeared, moving directly toward the anchored schooner at a high rate of speed, as if riding the crest of a huge wave that wasn't there. According to the later testimony of crew members, the ghost ship passed close by the schooner's bow and faded away into a gray, fog-like mist.

Of course, no one believed the crew's preposterous

story at the time. Some people believed that the divers were murdered by the rest of the crew after they recovered the sunken gold. But since there was absolutely no evidence that any of the crew was not telling the truth, no one was ever brought to trial in the case.

Then, in the late 1950s, another salvage operation was attempted. It too was unsuccessful—and again the crew aboard the salvage craft underwent the terrifying experience of almost being run down by a runaway ghost ship which may or may not have been the *Flying Dutchman*.

A similar incident occurred in the western Pacific Ocean just before 1900. The steamship *Hannah Regan* sank in a storm off the coast of Okinawa. Like the *General Grant* some forty years before, the *Hannah Regan* had been carrying a diverse cargo, including more than one million dollars in gold.

A salvage company attempted to retrieve the gold from the wrecked *Hannah Regan*—but again the *Flying Dutchman* was sighted during the salvage operation. This time, though, her appearance was witnessed by the captain himself.

By now, the story should be familiar: a clear moonlit night, the sea still and calm, the captain on deck enjoying the tranquil evening after a hard day's work, when suddenly he noticed a strange, shadowy shape in the distance. The shadow soon resolved itself into an approaching sailing vessel which was, in the captain's words, "of a type which had not sailed the seas for two hundred years." Although its sails were furled (and therefore useless), the ship was moving toward the salvage craft at a high rate of speed, as if borne along by strong winds and heavy seas. The phantom ship came on, with the skeleton of its bare masts and rigging clearly visible in the bright moonlight, until it passed close beside the astonished captain's salvage boat and disappeared beneath the ocean's surface.

The following day, two divers drowned while working aboard the wrecked *Hannah Regan,* and the rest of the salvage operation was cancelled. Neither the captain nor his crew dared to face further misfortune at the hands of Captain Van der Decken and the *Flying Dutchman.*

In March, 1939, nearly one hundred swimmers and sunbathers at Glencairn Beach, South Africa, watched in mounting horror and fascination as a sailing ship suddenly appeared, driving at full sail toward certain destruction on the shore. Its sails billowed and tossed with the force of powerful trailing winds, although the surrounding seas were calm and there was no wind to fill the sails. The witnesses cried out and tried frantically to wave the ship away from its cruel fate. On it came, though, heedless of the spectators' futile warnings, churning through the waters of the Cape of Good Hope like a raging bull. And just as everyone on the beach was certain that the ship could go no farther without running aground—it vanished.

In September, 1942, four people at Mouille Point in Cape Town, South Africa reported having seen an incredibly old and battered sailing ship appear from out of the blue, heading for nearby Table Bay. When, after a quarter of an hour, the strange ship finally passed out of sight behind an island, the witnesses made inquiries and were told that there had been no sailing vessels of the type they described in the area for at least three hundred years.

Does the phantom ship known as the *Flying Dutchman* actually exist? Is she, as the legends suggest, a deadly apparition that has been cursed with having to sail the seas forever in search of victims to satisfy her captain's endless malice? Or is she just that—a legend, and nothing more—created by sailors anxious to justify their frequent (and sometimes fatal) mistakes and accidents at sea?

No one knows for sure, of course. But our world is filled with mysteries that people thus far have been unable to solve or to explain. It is not enough to pretend that the mysteries do not exist, simply because we cannot solve them.

Perhaps there *is* a *Flying Dutchman* out there somewhere, lashed and buffeted by the same stormy seas and gale force winds that have accompanied her on her lonely journey for the past four hundred years. And maybe she *does* carry the curse of the doomed for those sailors who are unfortunate enough to meet her on the high seas.

One thing is for sure: even the least superstitious of sailors would rather *not* see her, than see her and hope and pray that what he saw was just his imagination, after all.

About the Author

Dr. William E. Warren is an educator who has taught at all levels from elementary school through university; he has also coached various sports and has been an athletic director and camp counselor. His own interest in mysterious and "unexplained" happenings, as well as his awareness of young people's love of the occult, led him to write this collection of accounts of weird but true events.

Dr. Warren's previous books for Prentice-Hall include three books of scary/humorous fiction stories presented in split sequence: *The Graveyard and Other Not-So-Scary Stories, The Thing in the Swamp and More Not-So-Scary Stories*, and *Footsteps in the Fog: Still More Not-So-Scary Stories*, all illustrated by Edward Frascino. Dr. Warren and his wife Louise live in Vidalia, Georgia, where he teaches world history.

About the Artist

Neil Waldman says he knew he was an artist before he could speak. Illustration is more than a job—it is his life. He has received numerous awards, including Graphics U.S.A. and the Society of Illustrators Award of Merit. His work for Prentice-Hall includes illustrating two previous collections of true "ghost" stories, *The Moving Coffins: Ghosts and Hauntings Around the World* and *Best True Ghost Stories of the 20th Century*, both written by David C. Knight. He is also the selector and illustrator of *Tales of Terror* by Edgar Allan Poe, also from Prentice-Hall. Mr. Waldman lives in Greenburgh, New York, with his wife Jeri and two children.

DATE DUE

OCT 5			

GAYLORD

PRINTED IN U.S.A.

13,046

001.9   Warren, William E.
W
        The headless ghost

C#1

$12.95

DATE			
MAR 21 '89	JAN 15 '93		
02 '9 ' 3			
	MAY 17 '93		
APR 11 '89	10-20-94		
JUN 8 '89	10129		
DEC 13 '90	11/12/03		
APR 22 '91			
MAR 4 '92			
SEP 18 '92			
JAN 15 '93			